The MODERN
Dolls' House

The MODERN Dolls' House

Jean Nisbett

Principal Photography by
Alec Nisbett

First published 2004 by
Guild of Master Craftsman Publications Ltd,
166 High Street, Lewes,
East Sussex, BN7 1XU

ISBN 1 86108 321 1

Patterns on pages 6, 7, 27, throughout Part 1 (28–80), 150 and 152 are from *William Morris, Designs and Patterns* by Norah Gillow, reproduced courtesy of Studio Editions, the pattern on page 81 and throughout Part 2 (82–110) is from *A Treasury of Design for Artists and Craftsmen* by Gregory Mirow, reproduced courtesy of Dover Publications.

Principal photography by Alec Nisbett
(Other photographs as acknowledged below)

Publisher: Paul Richardson
Art Director: Ian Smith
Production Manager: Stuart Poole
Managing Editor: Gerrie Purcell
Commissioning Editor: April McCroskie
Editor: Dominique Page
Designer: Danny McBride
Illustrator: John Yates
Typeface: Swiss, Gill sans

Colour origination by CTT Repro

Printed and bound by Stamford Press Pte Ltd (Singapore)

Photo acknowledgements
Jean Nisbett and the Guild of Master Craftsman Publications gratefully acknowledge the following people and agencies for granting permission to reproduce their photographs in this book. The photographs on the following pages were supplied courtesy of: Wendy Allin Miniatures 110, Angus Puffins 108, 116 (bottom right), Marie-France Beglan 40 (top right), 45 (top right), David Booth 43 (bottom left), Alan Borwell (of Borcraft Miniatures) 89 (top right), J C Brown (of Edwardian Elegance) 43 (top right), 44, Neil Carter 50 (main picture), Henry J Colbert (of Colbert Designs) 51 (main picture), Jeremy Collins (of Gable End Designs) 62, 63, 64 (arranged by Helen Zetter), 82 (bottom), 99 (centre) and 101, The Dolls House Emporium 30, 31 (bottom), 32, 35, 36, 46, 52 and 53 (bottom), back cover, Judith Dunger (photographs by Trevor Dunger) 95, Frances H England (of England's Magic) 40 (bottom), A G Funnell (of Lenham Pottery Models) 45 (bottom), GMC Publications (photograph by Chris Skarbon) 53 (centre), (photograph by Manny Cefai) 59 (top), (photographs by Chris Skarbon) 63 (bottom), 109 (bottom), (photograph by Colin Entwhistle) 109 (top), James Hemsley (of Trigger Pond Dolls Houses) 112, Ian Holoran (photographs by Colin Brown) 34, The London Dolls House Company (photographs by Giles Stokoe, front cover, 47 (bottom), 48 (top), 77, 79 (bottom) and 88 (centre) (furniture by Kim Selwood), 89 (bottom), 90, 105, 114 (top right) (kitchens by ELF), Catherine Munière 69 (bottom), George Parker (of Elphin Dolls Houses) 47 (top), 55 (bottom), Kenneth and Kay Rawding (photograph by Kenneth Rawding) 53 (top left), Colin and Yvonne Roberson (photographs by Yvonne Roberson) 55 (top), 102 (bottom right), Christopher Rouch (of Toptoise Design) 27, 31 (top right), 33, 87 (top right), 106, Kim Selwood (photograph by Mary-Jane Selwood) 37, M E Shaw (of Delph Miniatures) 82 (top right), P M Venning (of Pat Venning Porcelain) 50 and 51 (border pictures), 61 (top), 67 (top).

For my family,
and especially for
THEO

CONTENTS

Imperial and Metric
The standard dolls' house scales are 1/12 and 1/24, both originally based on imperial measures: in 1/12, one inch represents one foot. Although many craftspeople now use metric measurements, dolls' house hobbyists in Britain and especially America still use feet and inches. In this book imperial measures of length are given first (with the exception of materials that are specifically supplied in metric), followed by their metric equivalent. Accuracy to the millimetre is generally inappropriate, and metric measurements are often rounded up or down a little for convenience.

ACKNOWLEDGEMENTS

I would like to thank April McCroskie for her initial encouragement and Gerrie Purcell for overseeing the project. Danny McBride and John Yates added greatly to the appearance of this book, and my editor, Dominique Page, sorted out many problems along the way. I acknowledge their work with gratitude, and also that of the whole team at Guild of Master Craftsman Publications.

Without the work of my husband, Alec, this book would not have come to fruition. A book of this kind depends largely on the quality of the photographs, and I am deeply grateful for all his hard work in taking so many pictures.

I would like to thank all the makers who loaned photographs of their work to reproduce in this book, and also those who loaned miniatures for us to photograph. Avon Miniatures, Box Clever Miniatures, Derek Clift, Judith Dunger, Elf, Glasscraft, Tony Knott, K T Miniatures, The Linen Press, The Luggage Lady, Carol Mann, McQueenie Miniatures, Ottervale China, Peppermint Designs, Seaside Miniatures, Lyndel and Leslie Smith and Jenny Till were all generous in this respect.

Special thanks are also due to two suppliers who provided additional photographs: The Dolls House Emporium and London Dolls House Company. I am also grateful to other suppliers who loaned miniatures for our photography: Carol Black Miniatures (Mail Order), The Heritage Doll Company, Margaret's Miniatures of Warminster, Caroline Nevill Miniatures of Bath, Small Sorts of Salisbury and A Woman's Touch.

This book would never have been published without the support of the craftspeople who make dolls' houses and miniatures to delight everyone who takes part in the hobby. I want to say thank you to all these makers, whether their work appears in this book or not, for their skills and dedication. The dolls' house hobby depends on them, as it does on the fair organizers and shop owners who present their work to the public.

INTRODUCTION

At the start of the twenty-first century, home decoration is a major preoccupation: television programmes and illustrated books proliferate to show the way, and miniaturists have begun to replicate modern interiors and to include the latest ideas in their small-scale rooms, rather than concentrate solely on period styles.

This book covers decorative styles from 1900 to the present day. I have included schemes to suit conventional dolls' houses of many different types, and individual room settings that provide plenty of alternatives. There are also terraces, patios and gardens.

In the past ten years, hobbyists have become more relaxed about scale. At one time, when a clear, common standard for both house and contents was still being established, 1/12 was promoted as the only acceptable scale by many leading miniaturists, but now 1/24 has become a popular alternative, especially for those with little space to display their collections. Even the smallest apartment can accommodate a variety of 1/24 projects, and individual room boxes in either scale take up less space than a conventional dolls' house.

You should have no difficulty in finding miniatures in your chosen scale to suit any modern scheme as, like the hobbyists, many professional miniaturists have diversified to make twentieth-century and ultra-modern furniture and accessories to complement their established period designs.

A period dolls' house, enriched by beautifully made furniture and accessories is a delight, but beyond that there are many exciting possibilities open to the miniaturist who wants to tackle something more up to date. With this in mind, I include suggestions on how to use economical materials for decoration and also how to adapt easily obtainable and inexpensive objects to make simple furniture.

Whether you choose to reproduce a scheme shown in this book or, following the principles described, are inspired to complete something unusual for yourself, I hope that you enjoy the process as much as I have. Designing and furnishing miniature rooms and outdoor settings for the twentieth and twenty-first centuries is an absorbing pastime – and there should be something here to suit all tastes.

PRACTICAL MATTERS

This introduction to tools, techniques and materials is intended as a guide to the beginner in the dolls' house hobby and as a reminder for the more experienced. I have also provided a checklist of paint colours and decorative features that are appropriate for key twentieth- and twenty-first-century styles.

TOOLS

You need the following simple tools to make and fit out a dolls' house or room box. They can be obtained from suppliers of art materials, good stationers or craft shops.

- A self-healing cutting mat marked with a squared grid.

- A craft knife with replaceable blades. If you are unsure how to change the blades safely, ask the supplier to demonstrate.

- A transparent plastic 18in (45cm) ruler for measuring.

- A metal ruler with a raised edge, for use as a cutting guide. It is worth paying a little more for a thick ruler designed for professional use, rather than a cheap one that may be flimsy.

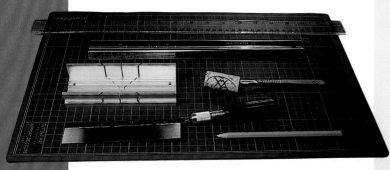

▲ Basic tools laid out on a cutting mat.

- A metal mini mitre box and saw to use for cutting stripwood or wooden mouldings, such as X-Acto mitre box No. 7533 and knife handle No. 5 fitted with saw blade No. 259. Other makes are available, all of a fairly standard size.

MITRED JOINS

The mitre box has both straight and angled slots for accurate cutting. The 45° angled cut is used to make corner joints; for example when fitting replica skirting board and picture rail in Edwardian and 1930s rooms, or for making fireplaces and picture frames.

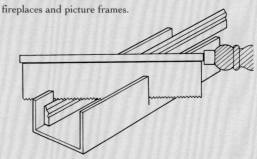

Fitting the corners of skirting board together.

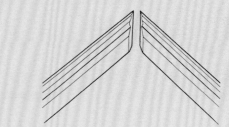

SAFETY FIRST

- Blades on craft knives must be changed frequently. They are inexpensive, and effective only when sharp – if blunt, the cut will not be accurate.

- To avoid accidents, always check before you cut that your free hand is behind the blade and not in front of it.

- Never use cutting tools when you are tired, as it then becomes all too easy to make mistakes. There is always another day.

- Always put a craft knife down while you check or adjust the position of the work. It is easy to forget that you are holding it and to nick yourself.

- Cutting tools are for use by adults only. Store a sharp blade safely by digging the end into a cork, and keep it out of the reach of children.

- Take extra care when cutting acetate sheet (for windows or see-through walls). This material is slippery and the knife can skid if not held firmly.

▲ Ready to cut window glazing.

ADHESIVES

Use the right glue for the purpose. Modern adhesives are not interchangeable.

ALL-PURPOSE CLEAR ADHESIVE
(E.G. UHU AND BOSTIK)
Use for card, paper, wood, ceramics, foamboard and clear acetate sheet. This type of adhesive bonds quickly but then needs to be left for a time until the glue has set firm. When joining wooden parts, tape them together with masking tape until the glue has set.

PVA WHITE WOOD ADHESIVE
(E.G. EVO-STIK RESIN 'W')
Use to make a permanent join: once the glue has set, the bond cannot be undone.

GLUE FUMES
Most glues give off fumes. It is therefore essential to work in a well-ventilated room, preferably with the window open. Keep strong glues away from children.

MODERN MATERIALS FOR MODERN DOLLS' HOUSES

FOAMBOARD
Foamboard can be used instead of wood to make a dolls' house or room box. It is easy to work with, inexpensive, and light in weight. It can be cut with a craft knife and glued together without the need for pins and screws, which makes it particularly suitable for the hobbyist who does not have a home workshop or advanced woodworking skills. The smooth surface takes paint well or it can be wallpapered. It is available in A4, A5 and also larger sizes. There are two thicknesses: 3.5mm (approx. ⅛in) and 5mm (approx. ⅛in), both of which are suitable for 1/24 and 1/12 scale constructions.

ACETATE SHEET
This is used for dolls' house window glazing or see-through walls or panels. It is available in A4 and A5 sizes from craft shops or suppliers of art materials, and there are several different thicknesses to choose from. It can be transparent, semi-opaque or coloured.

PLASTICIZED ENVELOPE STIFFENER
This is another useful material for providing 'glass' walls, roofs or partitions for modern rooms. It is semi-transparent and has a reeded appearance. A thicker, opaque black version can be useful for flooring. This is available from some craft shops and stationers that stock educational materials.

BALSA WOOD
Balsa can be used as a base shape; for example to make a fireplace. It has a tendency to crumble but can be cut with a saw blade with care. It does not take paint or varnish satisfactorily and should, in general, only be used when it will be covered with card or plasticized paper.

CUTTING NOTES
All these materials can be cut with a craft knife on a cutting mat, against a metal ruler with a raised edge. Envelope stiffener can also be cut with scissors, using the ridges as a guideline.

NOTES ON GLUEING
All-purpose, clear adhesive works well on all these materials. Run a trail of glue along one edge only, leave

it to get tacky, then press the edges to be joined firmly together. Hold for a minute or two to secure a bond. When joining foamboard walls, tape them together with masking tape until the glue has set firm.

Acetate seems to attract glue, which can inadvertently streak across the surface. When fitting glazing, use a wooden cocktail stick to apply a minimal amount of glue around the edges of the recess. When this is tacky, position the acetate over the window space and press it firmly into place in one movement. If the worst happens, glue streaks can be removed with white spirit before the glue has set.

Both acetate and envelope stiffener will bond firmly in seconds.

MAKE A ROOM BOX

It may be helpful to try out initial ideas in a simple room box before deciding on a final scheme. Buy an inexpensive, ready-made box or make your own. Either way, it will be easy to change the arrangement, and also to reuse the box later on if you wish. On the other hand, you may like your first idea so much that you decide to keep it as it is and decorate the exterior of the box to complement the scheme.

Here are two styles of room box: the measurements can be adapted to either scale.

DESIGN 1:
Two-sided open room box in 1/24

1 Cut the walls and floor from 3.5mm (approx. ⅛in) foamboard as indicated, using the lines on a cutting mat as a guide to make sure that the edges are parallel and the corners square.

2 Glue the foamboard pieces together following the sequence shown.

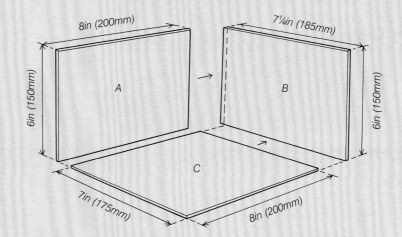

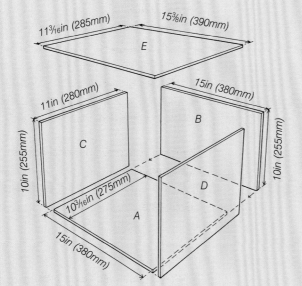

DESIGN 2:
Three-sided room box in 1/12

1 Measure and cut pieces from 5mm (¼in) foamboard as indicated.

2 Glue the pieces together, following the sequence shown.

If preferred, the ceiling can be added after interior decorations are complete; this will make access easier.

DECORATIONS

Try to keep an open mind when planning decorations, and avoid becoming too set on one scheme initially. Depending on what paints and materials you collect, you may find you like a colour combination you had not previously considered. Before you decide, lay out a selection of materials to check how colours, textures and patterns look when placed together in the small space of a dolls' house room.

Once you have gained experience by making and decorating a room box, you may decide to begin on a whole house. Instructions and plans to make two modern homes, both using foamboard as the main construction material, one in 1/24 and one in 1/12, are given later (see pages 70–80). I also show how to make a small modern town house by assembling boxes, with no tools required (see pages 114–115).

Whether you decide to buy a ready-made house, assemble one from a kit or make your own, decorating and furnishing the miniature rooms is guaranteed to give hours of pleasure.

Here is a brief guide to paint colours and typical features for twentieth- and twenty-first-century exteriors and interiors that can be simulated in small scale.

> **Hint**
>
> Art mounting board is available in a wide range of colours. Finishes include plain, matt colours, textured or satin, and some pale colours are mottled. To avoid painting, simply use mounting board to make inner walls in a room box in the colour of your choice. Fix these walls in place securely with double-sided Scotch tape along all the edges. This idea is particularly useful in an experimental room, where you might wish to change the decorative scheme at a later date.

SUITABLE PAINT COLOURS AND FINISHES FOR HOUSE EXTERIORS

ART NOUVEAU

Walls	Stone or brick with coloured or gilded decoration and lettering.
Features	Large windows with leaded lights or stained glass. Ornamental cast-iron balconies in curvilinear designs. Round-headed porches with mosaic tiles.

GLASGOW SCHOOL

Walls	White or pale grey traditional Scottish 'harled' (textured) finish.
Roof	Grey slate.
Paintwork	White.
Features	Oak front door with stone lintel. Small-paned windows.

ARTS AND CRAFTS

Reuse of earlier period houses with new features inside.
Cottage style favoured.

Features	Handmade ironwork door furniture.

EDWARDIAN

Walls	Brick.
Roof	Red slate with white barge boarding on gables.
Features	Mock-Tudor timbers, verandah or conservatory. Oak or white-painted front door. Porch with stained-glass insets and black and white or coloured tile floor.

ART DECO

Walls	White or pastel-coloured.
Roof	Green tiled or flat.
Features	Front door with tiled floor to porch, stained-glass insets. Sunray-design garden gate.

TRADITIONAL STYLE: 1920s–1930s

Walls	Stone or brick, sometimes pebble-dash.
Roof	Red or grey slate.
Paintwork	White, often green on smaller homes.
Features	Oak front door, sometimes studded, painted green or white on smaller homes. Quarry-tiled porch.

THE WARTIME YEARS: 1940s

Walls and roof	Prefabricated houses. Corrugated sheets.
Features	Small front garden.

1950s–1960s

	Architect-designed concrete houses and apartment blocks.
Roof	Flat with roof terrace.
Features	Front door painted in bright colour: deep blue, purple, yellow or red.

1970s–1990s

	As above but more use of brick and glass. Conversions in old agricultural and industrial buildings.

2000–PRESENT DAY

	Reinvention of Georgian two- or three-storey town house with much use of glass.
Features	White exteriors on newbuild homes. Roof terrace or roof garden.

SUITABLE PAINT COLOURS AND MATERIALS FOR INTERIORS

ART NOUVEAU

Walls	Elaborate wallpaper with swirly patterns. Frieze below ceiling.
Floors	Polished wood. Art Nouveau carpet designs (unfitted).
Paintwork	Off-white or dark-coloured.
Features	Fireplaces with copper or pewter ornamentation, brick hearths. Tiffany-style glass ornaments and lights. Copper, pewter and silver ornaments.

GLASGOW SCHOOL

Walls	White. Stylized stencil decoration in rose design.
Floors	Plain, pale carpet or wood with small carpet having stylized motif.
Paintwork	White. Occasionally very dark, almost black.
Features	Gesso (plaster) wall plaques. High-backed chairs (Mackintosh's own design). Coloured glass, where possible (e.g. light fittings, small insets in doors and furniture).

ARTS AND CRAFTS

Walls	Plain cream with wall hangings: tapestries or heavy curtains.
Floors	Planked oak with rugs.
Paintwork	Oak grain.
Features	William Morris and C. F. A. Voysey fabrics. Oak furniture. Hand-beaten copper and pewter ornaments.

EDWARDIAN

Walls	Patterned wallpapers (floral or striped). Deep frieze below ceiling. Wooden panelling.
Floors	Polished wood or linoleum, topped with patterned carpet square, leaving the surround bare.
Paintwork	White or stained medium oak
Features	Fireplace with elaborate mantelshelf and mirror above, grate with tiled surround. Occasional tables. A piano. Picture rail and gilt-framed paintings. Reproduction furniture from many periods.

ART DECO

Walls	Wallpaper with avant-garde 1930s designs or the 'all-white' look. (Off-whites.)
Floors	Pale, wall-to-wall carpet.
Paintwork	White.
Features	Chinese carpets and screens. Clarice Cliff pottery, figurines in bronze, ivory or ceramic, depicting movement.

TRADITIONAL STYLE: 1920s–1930s

Walls	Cream, sometimes textured in lounge and hall. Pink or pale blue in bedrooms. Half-tiled in kitchens and bathrooms, green and cream or black and white.
Floors	Stained oak with patterned carpet square.
Paintwork	Cream or grained oak.
Features	Standard lamps, flying ducks on wall, pottery ornaments.

THE WARTIME YEARS: 1940s

'Make do and mend'.

Accesories	Identity cards, station books, gas mask boxes, newspapers with war headlines.

1950s

Walls	One wall papered as a feature, and the others plain.
Floors	Fitted carpet in bright colours.
Paintwork	White.
Features	New 1950s fabric designs for curtains and upholstery. Coffee table. Pale furniture with Scandinavian influence, or new moulded plastic chairs and tables.

1960s–1970s

Walls	Plain colours becoming brighter through this period with purple and turquoise. Hessian used on small areas of wall.
Floors	Fitted carpet.
Paintwork	White.
Features	Hi-fi (record player and long-playing vinyl records). Corner armchairs and low unit seating. Wall-hung shelving. Shag-pile carpets in 1970s.

1980s

Walls	Laura Ashley-style floral wallpapers.
Floors	Fitted carpet, plain colours.
Paintwork	White.
Features	The country-house 'look', with antiques. Large sofas. Brocade curtains with tie-backs. Pine or hand-painted kitchen furniture. The Aga cooker (status symbol). Spongeware pottery, baskets used as accessories.

1990s–PRESENT DAY

Walls	Plain, pale colours.
Floors	Pale wood, rugs.
Paintwork	White.
Features	Calm, Zen-influenced interiors. Oriental accessories and ornaments. Ultra-modern kitchens with stainless steel appliances. The universally pale, minimalist look. Delicate flower-printed fabrics and wallpapers.

FURNITURE

In any period interior you will want to include exact reproductions of beautiful designs in the correct style for the time. For example, look at the elegant furniture based on pieces by Charles Rennie Mackintosh (see pages 33–35) or the pretty furniture in the Edwardian rooms (see pages 41–44). Furniture made by professional miniaturists also features in the 1950s houses in shapes that would be difficult to copy, unless you have skills well above the average, as the originals were made of moulded plastic.

ECONOMICAL IDEAS

Low-cost furniture can be made to look stunning by choosing a suitable paint finish. Many pieces of inexpensive imported furniture are supplied too thickly varnished, but the shapes are good and the finish can be transformed.

The first step is to remove the varnish with a proprietary paint stripper, using wire wool and an old toothbrush to reach into the corners. Cover the work surface with layers of newspaper, wear rubber gloves to protect your hands and keep windows open for good ventilation. Wipe the piece over with white spirit and leave it on a window sill so that the smell evaporates. Then repaint with satin-finish model enamel.

My example is a French-style armoire – a capacious cupboard fitted with shelves that can be used to store linen or kitchen crockery in a period or modern home. To use in a bedroom, choose a pale colour, perhaps an off-white or a delicate green.

◄ Before:
The over-glossy finish is unsuitable in a dolls' house.

▼ After:
Painted in a mid-green, this armoire is ideal for a kitchen. Line the shelves with wallpaper with a small pattern to set off crockery or linen.

▼ Plain, wooden furniture can be painted with model enamel. Here are some simple pieces repainted in bold colours that will show up well in an all-white modern room.

SIMPLE FURNITURE TO MAKE

More recently, high-quality furniture has tended to rely on clean lines and good colours for effect. For the hobbyist who enjoys making dolls' house furniture, it is not difficult to copy some of these designs at very little expense. Simple shapes can be adapted to suit many modern schemes by choosing an appropriate wood stain or paint colour or, in the case of upholstered chairs or sofas, by finding a suitable fabric to use as a covering.

Here are some basic pieces to give you a start; you are sure to think of others. These will help to complete a room setting or fill in a gap when you cannot find exactly the size of table or bed you require, and you can choose the finish to complement your scheme.

▶ A transparent plastic box will simulate a modern glass table.

A PLASTIC TABLE WITH ATTACHED SEAT

1 For the table, use a plastic box that is approximately 2in (50mm) L x 1½in (40mm) W x 1½in (40mm) H, or a square one if preferred. Small boxes used as containers for jewellery or miniatures come in a range of sizes and you may find one that is appropriate.

2 Cut a block of wood to the same size and paint or stain it. Then, pad the top of the seat with a piece of foam covered with any suitable fabric.

3 Fix the seat to the table with double-sided Scotch tape.

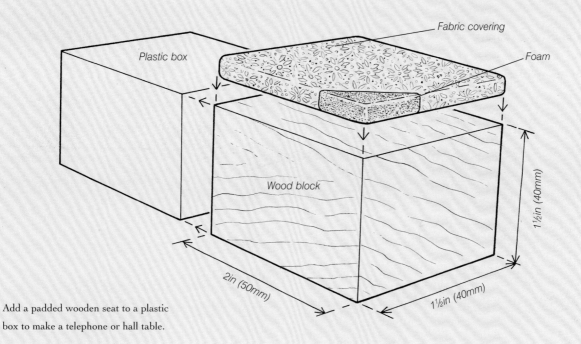

Add a padded wooden seat to a plastic box to make a telephone or hall table.

A PLAIN MODERN TABLE

1 To make the table, use ¼in (6mm) thick, smooth wood – jelutong or mahogany is best.

2 Cut the pieces to the measurements shown. Glue the pieces together.

3 Stain and polish or varnish with satin-finish varnish.

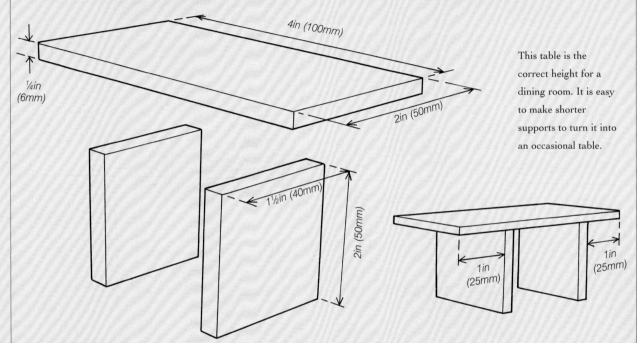

This table is the correct height for a dining room. It is easy to make shorter supports to turn it into an occasional table.

4in (100mm)

¼in (6mm)

2in (50mm)

1½in (40mm)

2in (50mm)

1in (25mm)

1in (25mm)

A BED

The measurements given are for a large, single bed. Extend the width to 5¼in (135mm) to make a double bed.

1 Use ½in (13mm) thick wood for the top and 1in (25mm) thick wood for the base. Cut and glue the pieces together as shown.

2 This design leaves a 'shelf' around the mattress or duvet. The bed and the base should be stained and polished or varnished in a suitable shade to suit your room.

The latest bed designs feature polished wood and a minimalist look. This style should be complemented by a duvet.

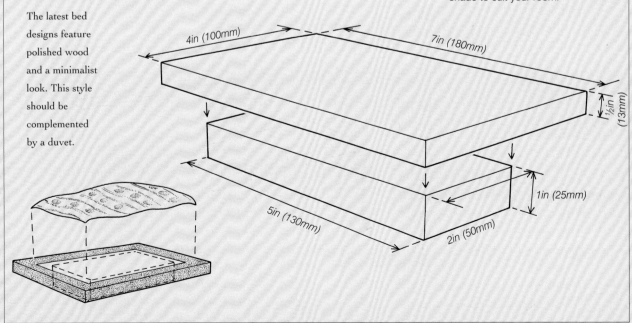

4in (100mm)

7in (180mm)

½in (13mm)

1in (25mm)

5in (130mm)

2in (50mm)

A CORNER SOFA UNIT

1 Use ⅜in (10mm) thick jelutong to make the sofa unit.

2 Cut the seat, back and side pieces to the measurements given. Glue the back to the back edge of the side piece to make an L-shape.

3 Cut the front leg from ⅜in (10mm) square dowel and glue to the front corner of the seat.

4 When the glue has set, glue the sofa base plus the leg into the corner unit. Stain and polish or varnish.

5 Pad the sofa seat with fabric-covered foam. Add matching or contrasting cushions.

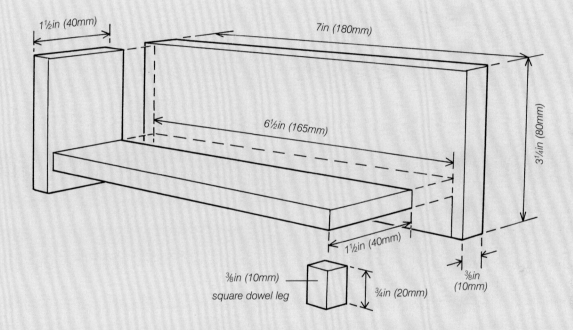

1½in (40mm)

7in (180mm)

6½in (165mm)

3¼in (80mm)

1½in (40mm)

⅜in (10mm)

⅜in (10mm)
square dowel leg

¾in (20mm)

A sofa unit can be fitted into the corner of a kitchen or study. Painted rather than stained and polished, this design could also be used as a bed for a child.

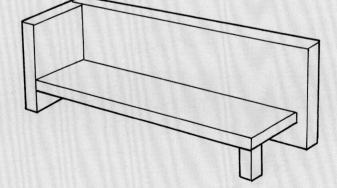

AN ARMLESS CHAIR COVERED WITH RIBBON OR BRAID

This style of chair is adaptable. The height given is suitable for a dining chair – make it lower to use in a bedroom or sitting room.

1 Cut the seat and back to the measurements shown. Glue the back to the seat, making sure the bases match exactly.

2 Cover with ribbon or braid as follows:

a) Spread glue thinly over the front and rear of the chair's back, and the top and front of the seat only. Starting at the base of the back, take the ribbon over the back and seat and glue underneath.

b) Spread glue on the sides of the seat. Then, starting under the base, take ribbon across and over the seat (covering the first layer of ribbon), and finishing underneath as before.

3 Slipstitch the edges of the ribbon together down the sides of the back.

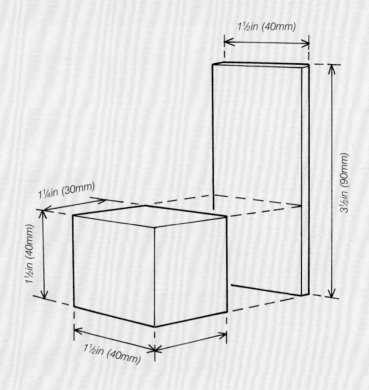

Slipstitch together to close gap

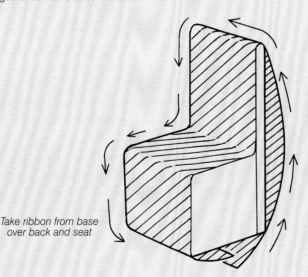

Take ribbon from base over back and seat

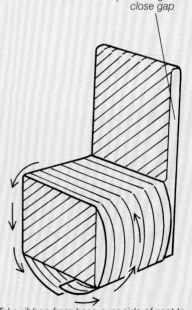

Take ribbon from base over side of seat to the other side, covering first piece of fabric in other direction

ACCESSORIES

Modern schemes can be completed on a modest budget by the use of a wide range of materials other than those made specifically for dolls' houses. If you find something inexpensive that you feel you will be able to adapt, do not hesitate to buy it – the opportunity may not occur again.

Be prepared to experiment and do some lateral thinking. Keep a file of pictures cut from magazines and brochures for use as backgrounds or scenes to be glimpsed through doorways or windows. Pictured carpets can look realistic, while pictures of tiles can be cut out, glued to card and then reassembled on floors or as a border on walls. Never throw away any oddments of wood: keep a box for off-cuts. Eventually, you may find a use for even the most unlikely-looking shape or size.

To create original ornaments for the modern room, use beads and small pieces of fancy braid and ribbon. Picture frames, iron-on motifs, children's hair ornaments, such as slides and bobbles, giftwrap and greetings cards, bottle tops, lids from jars, small boxes, corks and fancy paper clips can all be used to make decorative accessories, and examples of such uses are shown throughout this book.

> **Hint**
> Some buttons have a sturdy-looking shank on the back, but often this is of plastic, not metal, and it can be cut off with a pair of wire-cutters so that the button back is flat, making it easier to attach to a wall or use as an ornament.

▲ Novelty buttons and trimmings have many uses. Those pictured here are all used to simulate light-fittings in this book.

EASY IDEAS

- An ornate classical fireplace can work surprisingly well in a minimalist room. Try an elaborate cast-resin model and see if you like the effect.

- Make two fireplaces by cutting a plain resin or wood picture frame in half and painting.

- Mantelshelves come into fashion periodically, such as in an Edwardian or 1980s room. They are useful in the dolls' house as a small display area for ornaments. Use plain stripwood to add a mantelshelf over a fireplace, but note that they were not fashionable in the 1930s when tiled fireplaces were favoured.

▲ Tablemats are available in a wide range of shapes and sizes, colours and textures.

- Use a cap from a scent bottle as a wastepaper bin.

- Tablemats have many uses: a coarse, raffia one can be used as flooring; small bamboo mats make good non-working window blinds (see page 124); a textured cloth mat can be used as a carpet; a bead mat will add sparkle to an Art Deco room; and a mosaic mat can become part of a courtyard or patio.

- Leather is generally too thick to work satisfactorily in small scale, but a cleaning cloth for spectacles, washed and smoothed out, will give a good simulation of suede for seating or bedspreads.

- To colour decorations or miniature picture frames gold, use a marker pen of the type that has to be shaken before and during use, and avoid the tedious task of cleaning a paintbrush.

ADD LIFE TO YOUR ROOM SETTINGS

A dolls' house without dolls may seem a contradiction. I have chosen to concentrate on design and decoration, but many hobbyists will want to enliven their interiors with some inhabitants. Professional makers of miniature dolls can provide characterful modern dolls in both 1/12 and 1/24. If you are neat-fingered, kits are also available to assemble and dress your own dolls in an individual way.

The secret of success when adding dolls to a scene is to pose them as though engaged in some occupation. Even two dolls having a conversation can bring extra life and interest to a room.

▲ This adorable pet is made in metal and hand painted. (From author's collection.)

PETS

Every miniature home needs a pet dog or cat. Be careful, though, to choose a suitable breed: pug dogs or pekinese were liked in the early part of the twentieth century; for a country house a retriever or a labrador might be best; Scottish and Sealyham terriers were popular in the 1930s; and for a home of today, simply choose your favourite.

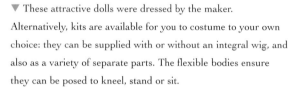

▼ These attractive dolls were dressed by the maker. Alternatively, kits are available for you to costume to your own choice: they can be supplied with or without an integral wig, and also as a variety of separate parts. The flexible bodies ensure they can be posed to kneel, stand or sit.

Early Twentieth-Century Decorative Styles

Part 1

THE ART NOUVEAU STYLE

Art Nouveau evolved towards the end of the nineteenth century and flourished well into the twentieth. Essentially a European style, it was taken up in America with enthusiasm but at that time was less appreciated in Britain, where more traditional buildings and furniture were generally favoured. Art Nouveau was a break with tradition, in sharp contrast to previous ideas.

It was followed in Europe by the modernists and Bauhaus, while in Britain the Arts and Crafts movement looked backward to medieval style but also placed the emphasis on handwork and the role of the individual craftsman in producing beautiful objects.

Art Nouveau decorations featured distinctive, stylized designs of plants and flowers on fabrics and wallpapers, elaborate metalwork on staircases and balustrades, and curvaceous furniture embellished with symbolist details. The façades of buildings were decorated with mosaic tiles, gilding and intricate cast-iron balconies that were sometimes painted green to resemble bronze.

AN ART NOUVEAU ROOM

▲ Hand-beaten pewter designed for Liberty, Tiffany-style glass and the essential vase of lilies accessorize this room appropriately.

This style is even more widely appreciated today, and you can have a lot of fun arranging such a room and enjoy the luxury of creating its extravagant decorations. My example has all the hallmarks: vivid green wallpaper, a parquet floor (in this room, floorpaper), partly covered by a rich-looking carpet. A characteristic fireplace incorporating beaten copper is from an inexpensive range of dolls' house furniture.

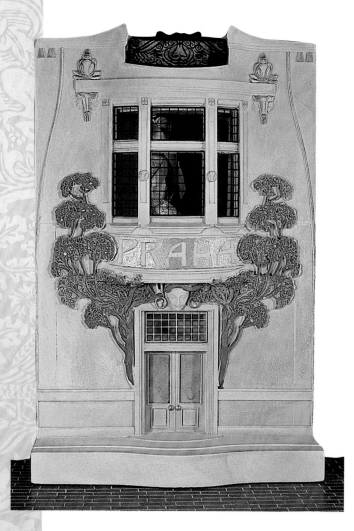

◀ This is a model of the elegant frontage of the Hotel Central in Prague, made in a very small scale to display on a mantelshelf or bookshelf. The area behind the balconied window provides a space that can be used to display a 1/24 figurine or sculpture.

◄The curvaceous screen and wall mirror with naturalistic, plant-like tendrils give this corner its distinctive Art Nouveau look. (Screen from author's collection.)

DECORATIVE ACCESSORIES

The style was both eccentric and elegant. Green was favoured as a colour for wallpapers and carpets. Pewter rivalled silver plate as a medium for ornamentation and craftsmanship, and Liberty of London marketed the work of leading designers, which sometimes incorporated enamel insets into pewter boxes.

ADD A PEACOCK FRIEZE

A deep frieze below the ceiling was often used as an additional decorative feature. Following the lead of Whistler's famous Peacock Room in America, completed in 1864, peacocks came to be seen as a symbol of Art Nouveau style, and were used both on friezes and in stained-glass panels through to the early years of the twentieth century.

◄The completed peacock frieze is effective and easy to create. Tiny, iridescent peacock stickers can be found in stationers and toy shops. Buy several packs to arrange on white, embossed paper to make a frieze that will enhance the room.

THE FEMININE TOUCH

Shopping, then as now, was a favourite pastime, especially for the lady of leisure who had both time and money to spend. Add a finishing touch to a room with some beautifully packaged purchases. Leave the lid next to a box to show off small items of clothing or a beautiful hat.

▼Attractive packaging that incorporates designs by Alphonse Mucha, the symbolist artist whose posters advertised exhibitions and much besides. Hat boxes were necessities, to protect the large, fragile hats of the time.

▼The silver-plated candlesticks on the mantelshelf are based on a turn-of-the-century Liberty design, while stained-glass insets in the firescreen are also typical of the period.

GLASGOW SCHOOL

The work of Charles Rennie Mackintosh, the Scottish architect and designer, key to the Glasgow School style, was much admired in Europe and has been linked with the Art Nouveau movement, but his houses and furniture were entirely individual. His tall, straight-backed chairs and sofas, based on interlaced willow adapted to a geometric grid pattern, are the antithesis of the flowing Continental style.

Sadly, he was commissioned to build few private houses in Britain, the best-known being Hill House in Helensburgh, near Glasgow, which is now owned by The National Trust for Scotland. This was his second, large Scottish house, the first being Windyhill, also near Glasgow, but many of his finest designs never left the drawing board.

Mackintosh's designs were influenced by Scottish castles, built to withstand gales and driving rain. In consequence, windows tend to be relatively small, the front door generally of solid oak, and walls are either of granite or stone or have a 'harled' finish (a typically Scottish textured render) that can be reproduced in miniature by mixing a small amount of interior filler into a matt, off-white paint. Ready-textured paints are also available in sample-size pots.

▼ A view of Gate Lodge, an attractive design for a house that was never built. The 1/24 dolls' house includes the massive chimney and tower that were features of Scottish fortified castles. This model was based on Mackintosh's original plans.

◀ This impressive house shows all the characteristics of Mackintosh's distinctive style.

The MODERN Dolls' House

Mackintosh's work did not become generally admired in his native Scotland until long after his death, but he is now accepted as one of the leading figures of twentieth-century architecture. Dolls' houses based on his designs appeal to modern hobbyists: they are straightforward to decorate and there are several makers who concentrate on Mackintosh-style houses and furniture in both 1/12 and 1/24.

▼ Mackintosh liked to use dark wood in an entrance hall to offer contrast to the white rooms that followed. The dark-stained pillars on this staircase are based on those at Hill House.

THE INTERIORS

A Mackintosh interior looks as modern today as when it was first decorated. In a dolls' house, mainly white rooms with pink and mauve accents and perhaps a frieze of his favourite stylized rose design (which can be assembled from cut-outs from a greetings card) will be effective and make an appropriate background for furniture based on his distinctive, decorative designs.

Dark furniture was often preferred in dining rooms and studies, sometimes even ebonized, but his preference for bedroom furniture was white with insets of coloured glass.

▼▶ The miniaturized Rose Boudoir chair is available in both 1/12 and 1/24. The original was designed by Mackintosh for an exhibition in Turin in 1902 and features stencilled decoration on the upholstered back and seat.

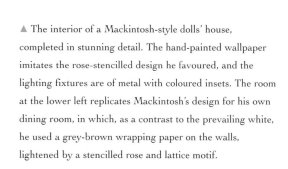

▲ The interior of a Mackintosh-style dolls' house, completed in stunning detail. The hand-painted wallpaper imitates the rose-stencilled design he favoured, and the lighting fixtures are of metal with coloured insets. The room at the lower left replicates Mackintosh's design for his own dining room, in which, as a contrast to the prevailing white, he used a grey-brown wrapping paper on the walls, lightened by a stencilled rose and lattice motif.

◄▲► The original Willow chair (top far right) was designed for Miss Cranston's Tea Rooms in Argyle Street, Glasgow, and is shown here with other chairs designed by Mackintosh.

◄▼► Bedroom furniture based on designs used in Hill House, with pink and purple glass insets.

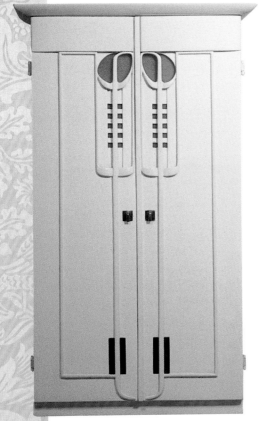

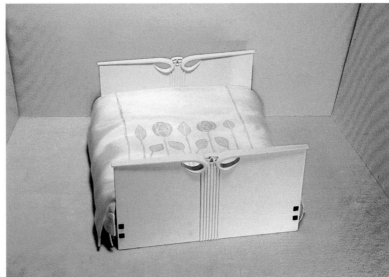

MAKE A MACKINTOSH ROOM

White walls make decorating a Mackintosh-style room a simple project. You may like to add a frieze – the one I placed near the fireplace was cut from a greetings card, but you can make your own by using a stencil or a soluble, coloured wax decorative material from a craft shop.

Mackintosh was strongly influenced by Japanese ideas, and in his own home, ornaments, although strictly limited in number, included Japanese vases, which sometimes contained an exquisite arrangement of delicate foliage.

If you plan a Mackintosh-inspired room, aim for the effect that an astonished visitor recorded on first seeing Mackintosh's own home in Glasgow: 'On the second floor of a modest building in the great industrial smoky town of Glasgow there is a drawing room amazingly white.'

▲ This room is sparsely furnished to show off my much-cherished 1/12 Mackintosh-style chairs, including an oak armchair. These particular pieces are no longer available but there is no shortage of similar furniture. The pale floor of a greyish-white card makes a good background for the needlepoint carpet, which can be worked from a kit.

▼ The centrepiece of the white-walled room is the beautiful fireplace, which incorporates shelves for ornaments.

THE ARTS AND CRAFTS HOME

Yet another style continued to develop in the early years of the twentieth century. William Morris's earlier insistence on quality and the work of the individual craftsman had led to the spread of the Arts and Crafts Movement. His own first married home, The Red House, was effectively the first Arts and Crafts house. It was built for him by his friend, the architect Philip Webb, of brick and oak, with medieval touches.

Edwin Lutyens also built individual homes that incorporated Tudor and Elizabethan features, and these were widely copied. His large, detached houses with generous gardens were built for wealthy clients, and

▲ Fireplaces in the Lutyens' dolls' house feature red brick, wide hearths and heavy oak mantelshelves. This imposing example has a hearth raised up by steps.

▼ A fine dolls' house that is available fully assembled or can be made from a kit. It has all the hallmarks of Lutyens' style: a magnificent oak-panelled door, tall Tudor chimneys with exterior chimneybreasts, and a red-tiled roof.

were often referred to as 'Tudorbethan'. Lutyens worked in collaboration with Gertrude Jekyll, who laid out the gardens to surround his houses, and he, in turn, designed garden furniture.

The American Arts and Crafts Movement also flourished. Frank Lloyd Wright built houses of concrete and steel but also lavished attention on handmade bricks, natural stone and slate, combining these with glass so that his houses seemed to be at one with the countryside.

The Arts and Crafts style works as well in a cottage as it does in a large Lutyens house. If you already have a Tudor dolls' house or a cottage, transforming the interior to feature the Arts and Crafts style could be an enjoyable project. Only minimal redecoration would be needed, as the key to this style is plain cream or off-white walls and wooden floorboards, stained as oak and left unpolished.

Frank Lloyd Wright designed his first Barrel chair around 1904 and refined the piece in a number of later versions. This striking 1/12 chair was made by an architect who also specializes in making miniatures of early twentieth-century furniture.

MAKE A FIREPLACE

The dominating feature of the rustic room is a large open fireplace. Like its predecessor, the inglenook, the Arts and Crafts version is designed to burn logs rather than coal, so needs to have an open hearth. The structural beam (a bressumer) over the earlier version is replaced by a hefty oak mantelshelf. Choose a slightly battered piece of wood or distress it, as it should not look too perfect. I found just what I wanted in my wood oddments box, a piece already sufficiently dented.

1 Make the fireplace from balsa wood or foamboard – build up layers if necessary to 1¼in (30mm) thick. Cut to size and cut out the central aperture to take the fire.

2 Cover the fireplace with stone-effect paper. Cut and fit the stripwood, painted black, along the inner edges of the grate aperture.

3 Make a hearth from thick card and cover with stone paper, wrapping it over to cover all the edges, then fix it to the floor with double-sided Scotch tape. (If preferred, the hearth can be tiled with realistic ceramic flagstones.)

4 Fit the fireplace over the hearth and glue to the wall. Glue the mantelshelf on top and to the wall.

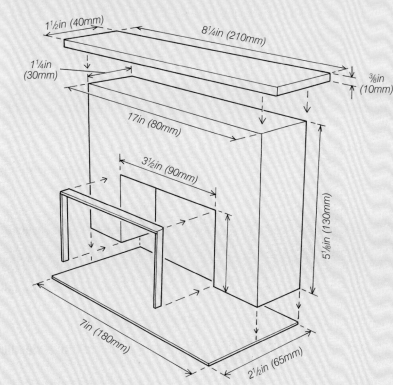

1½in (40mm)
8¼in (210mm)
1¼in (30mm)
⅜in (10mm)
1⅞in (80mm)
3½in (90mm)
5⅛in (130mm)
7in (180mm)
2½in (65mm)

Wooden planking rather than floor paper will add to the authentic look of the room. Iron-on oak planks are available in several widths – I recommend using the widest. Make a paper pattern of the floor first and cut it out in thin card to ensure a good fit. Then follow the maker's instructions for ironing on the planks, starting at the front of the room to give a neat edge.

When complete, glue the floor into the house with wood adhesive. Weigh down the floor overnight to ensure that it remains in place until the glue has set, so that the corners do not warp upwards. A pile of books can be useful for this purpose.

▼ Arts and Crafts enthusiasts favoured fresh air and the simple life. A window that opens will reinforce this impression. Inexpensive ready-made window frames are widely available. Curtains of William Morris fabric are suitable – use Liberty dress fabric which features patterns reduced in size from those on the original furnishing fabrics.

FURNITURE

Much of the Arts and Crafts furniture was made in the country rather than in town. In England, craftsmen migrated from London and set up workshops with the ideal of a simple life and closeness to nature. The English Cotswolds was chosen by C.R. Ashbee, the silversmith, to start his Guild of Handicrafts, but sadly the enterprise petered out after six years. It did, however, lay a solid foundation for good-quality craftwork in the Cotswolds which continues to this day.

▶ Made in oak, this miniature version of a Cotswold-style dresser with panelled doors is similar to those made by Ernest Gimson and Sidney Barnsley, who set up workshops in the English Cotswolds.

▲ Voysey's signature motif, the heart-shaped cut-out, appeared on refectory tables flanked by benches rather than chairs. This Arts and Crafts look was artistic, but like the medieval designs it reflected, not necessarily comfortable.

The furniture was plain but beautifully crafted and finished. There were oak or elm tables with stretchers imitating the shape of a ploughshare, country chairs in styles that had been followed for centuries, and oak dressers with panelled doors that suited the English cottage. And home interior styles followed; soon this English cottage look was what everyone wanted, even if they lived in town.

Heal's, one of the leading London furniture makers, began to produce store catalogues featuring their cottage-style furniture in 1905. An oak dresser was considered essential, and one could be bought for £6 15s.

The English cottage could be drafty, and heavy curtains were sometimes hung on walls in the manner of tapestries of earlier times. I included a picture of a well-known design by C.F.A. Voysey on one wall of my room to simulate such a hanging and add colour to the interior. Stoneware pottery is a good choice for the table, with mugs rather than frivolous cups and saucers.

ACCESSORIES

Hand-wrought silver, pewter and copper were plainer than Art Nouveau designs. Homeowners took up metalwork and woodwork as practical hobbies. The 'copper' plaque over the fireplace in this room came from a greetings card.

Remember not to over-furnish an Arts and Crafts room. A few simple pieces are all that is required to convey the atmosphere of the time.

▼ The copper picture frame and pewter candlesticks were copied from original Arts and Crafts designs by a professional miniaturist whose speciality is metalwork.

THE EDWARDIAN ERA

King Edward VII's short reign lasted only for the first decade of the twentieth century but Edwardian style had great influence on the way in which the ordinary British home was decorated and furnished for many years to follow. A pretty, light look gradually took over from the cluttered interiors prevalent at the end of Queen Victoria's reign: the average homemaker was not adventurous enough to follow the lead given by Charles Rennie Mackintosh, who was working at this time.

Many urban London families moved to the newly built suburbs on the outskirts, where they could live close to the countryside and have their own garden. Moving to a new house was a wonderful experience after the cramped conditions in many old Victorian town houses; it was also an opportunity to change the furniture and make a fresh start.

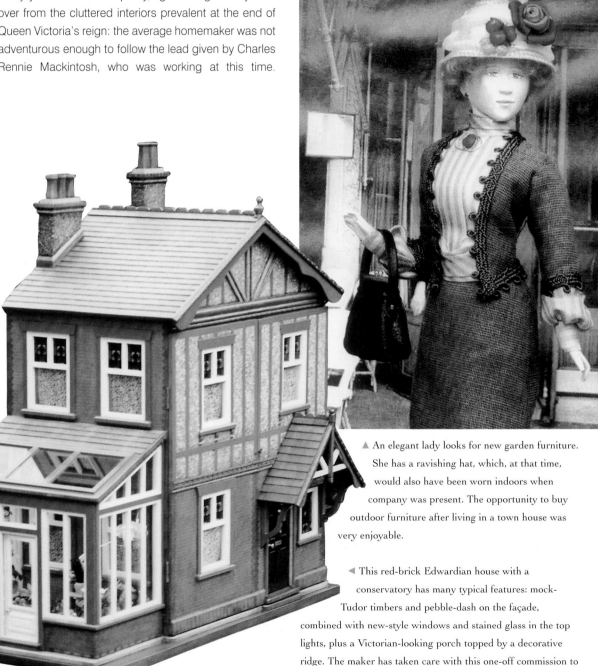

▲ An elegant lady looks for new garden furniture. She has a ravishing hat, which, at that time, would also have been worn indoors when company was present. The opportunity to buy outdoor furniture after living in a town house was very enjoyable.

◀ This red-brick Edwardian house with a conservatory has many typical features: mock-Tudor timbers and pebble-dash on the façade, combined with new-style windows and stained glass in the top lights, plus a Victorian-looking porch topped by a decorative ridge. The maker has taken care with this one-off commission to get every detail exactly right.

An Edwardian parlour was, above all, comfortable. Everything was of the best quality the householder could afford, and was looked after carefully. Even in the smaller home there was usually a daily maid to cope with cleaning and the all-important polishing. If you enjoy dolls you could include a maid in her frilly cap and apron, perhaps wielding a feather duster.

▲ The delicate floral wallpaper sets the tone for this pretty room.

◄ Conservatory furniture in painted metal. The Edwardians liked reproductions of earlier styles: the elegant chair is derived from early nineteenth-century Chinoiserie and the double seat has Gothic details. These handmade pieces are available in both 1/12 and 1/24.

FIT A FIREPLACE

The focal point of the parlour was still the fireplace, which was often a reproduction of an earlier style. The one in this parlour can be made from a kit with the additional option of a fireback to fit into a chimneybreast. Adding a chimneybreast to surround the fireplace provides convenient alcoves on either side for shelves and ornaments, a chair or a bookcase, and makes the whole room more interesting. A plainer, modern look does not suit the Edwardian room.

1 Cut the chimneybreast from balsa wood or build up layers of foamboard by glueing them together to reach the required thickness. The chimneybreast should be the full height of the room, deep enough to take the fireback and ¾in–1in (20–25mm) wider at each side than the fireplace.

2 Cut an aperture for the grate, using a craft knife. Check that the fireplace fits well, so that it can be pushed into place after wallpapering the room and chimneybreast. Paper across the grate aperture, and use a craft knife to trim the paper neatly when the paste has dried out.

SKIRTING BOARD AND PICTURE RAIL

Fit skirting boards and picture rails in an Edwardian room. These follow the Victorian moulding style and can be bought from dolls' house shops that stock DIY materials, or by mail order. Remember to mitre the corners, using a mitre box and saw (see Practical Matters, page 10). An off-white paint suits the period better than a modern, brilliant white, which can be toned down by adding a few drops of cream or ivory model enamel or acrylic to give it a creamy tone.

The picture rails were well used. Over the fireplace an overmantel mirror was obligatory, typically oval in shape and suspended by gilt chain from the rail. Small watercolour paintings of sentimental subjects, such as children in an idealized country setting, are appropriate. Reproductions of paintings by artists such as Helen Allingham can be cut from magazines or print catalogues and framed in gilt.

FLOORING AND FABRICS

Fit parquet flooring, either in wood or simulated by using a plasticized paper sheet. A carpet square in a floral or

◀ A tall plant-stand with elegantly curved legs shows off a green plant.

▼ This setting shows the pleasant effect of well-chosen furniture on a parquet floor. It is a rearrangement of the parlour furniture as it might have been used in an entrance hall, where the low narrow seat with striped silk covering was a useful item of furniture. To complete this scene, the large, handsome oil painting is hung low over the seat, rather than from the picture rail above.

Turkish pattern, or several rugs, should cover part of the floor, leaving a wooden surround. Curtains were floor-length, often in striped silk or damask, hung from wooden curtain poles. Miniature curtain sets can be bought complete with pole, finials and curtain rings. Alternatively, make poles from thin wood dowel, stain them medium oak or walnut, and use small gilt jewellery rings as curtain rings and beads as finials.

PARLOUR FURNITURE

Furnish the parlour with a plethora of fragile-looking occasional tables with crochet or tatted mats to protect the surfaces. Chairs can copy Sheraton style, or you might like to include a reproduction Knole sofa. Add a footstool or two and a piano for evening entertainment.

▼ A 1/12 piano copied from a Victorian model which bore the date 1889 on the key that opened the case. It is made from burr walnut, pine, lime and mahogany to give a rich effect, and the keys are recycled ebony and ivory. It is typical of many that would have remained in Edwardian homes at the dawn of the twentieth century, treasured and kept for sentimental reasons, rather than being replaced by newer models.

► The perfect dressing table for the Edwardian bedroom.

THE BEDROOM

Bedrooms were decorated with pretty floral wallpapers, silk curtains and lacy accessories. Furniture could be fussy: the most elaborate pieces included fretwork, and the Edwardian dressing table might have a large mirror topped with a Chippendale-style pediment and swing mirrors on either side. Whether plain or fancy, it was usually made of mahogany.

Even mass-produced furniture was well made and durable. In 1903, you could buy a bedroom suite of dressing chest, wardrobe and washstand for £8 10s and it would last a lifetime. The bed cost extra!

For children's and maids' bedrooms, plainer white-painted furniture was favoured. It looked clean and fresh and, unlike polished mahogany, could be wiped over easily with a damp cloth to remove fingermarks.

Central heating had not yet arrived for the average home, and bedrooms were very cold. This was considered healthy, and a window was

always left open at night to let in extra fresh air. A thick eiderdown was essential for comfort, usually made in silk or satin with a quilted pattern. One placed over the 'counterpane' (the term used before 'bedspread' was adopted) will make a decorative addition to the bed.

◀ ▼ A capacious wardrobe with delicate decoration has two deep drawers at the base as well as hanging space. The classic bedstead with wire base is fitted with brass castors. The details on these miniatures were reproduced from top-quality furniture of the period.

▼ ▶ A single wardrobe with a drawer, and a dressing chest topped with a swing mirror in a simple style. Although plain, the mirror frame and the detailing on the wardrobe indicate that these pieces are of fine quality.

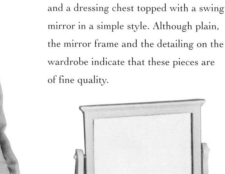

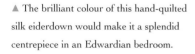

▲ The brilliant colour of this hand-quilted silk eiderdown would make it a splendid centrepiece in an Edwardian bedroom.

A BATHROOM

When you allocate room functions in an Edwardian dolls' house, unlike those from earlier periods, you can at last include a bathroom. Many households still had a washstand with ewer (a large jug with a wide mouth) and basin in the corner of the bedroom, and if your house is small then this is the option to choose. Even huge country houses might have only one or at most two bathrooms for the family, while for weekend guests the washing facilities remained severely limited.

Add plenty of accessories to the bathroom: a wooden towel 'horse', glass shelves on gilt or wooden brackets to hold toiletries, and a soap dish to hang over the edge of the bath are decorative. A bath mat with the word 'bath' can be worked from a needlepoint kit in stranded cotton. If you are short of time or do not enjoy needlework, a good substitute is to make a bath mat from a piece of facecloth and print 'BATH' using a black ballpoint pen.

An Edwardian dolls' house or room setting can look really delightful; it should be pretty, neat and homely. Finish the room with your own personal choice of ornaments and embroideries, but not too many, as much Victorian clutter had been swept away with the beginning of the new century.

▼ This charming bathroom has a high-flush water closet. Brass taps are fitted on the free-standing bath and the deep washbasin, and a potted palm emphasizes the period room style.

▲ These two elegant ladies are dressed to pay an afternoon call. They could be posed entering or leaving a house, apparently deep in conversation.

ART DECO

A radical new style always feels fresh, exciting, and at the cutting-edge of modern design, and none was more so than Art Deco, originally known as the Moderne style. It flourished during the 1920s and 1930s, and was introduced to a global public at the 1925 Paris Exhibition of Decorative Art, from which it gained its eventual name.

Art Deco was taken up rapidly in America, especially in California where flat-roofed houses with curving walls, roof terraces and light, spacious interiors were built along the West Coast. There the climate was ideal for sun roofs that could actually be used; in Britain, the true Art Deco house is a comparative rarity, as they sat less easily in a grey landscape with frequent rain. Flat roofs tend to leak and were viewed with suspicion – rightly so, from a practical point of view.

The style was particularly successful when used for apartment blocks and hotels, where the structure was large enough to show off the exterior decoration. On Miami Beach, such hotels have been restored and painted afresh in vibrant combinations of turquoise, pink and mauve, and, once again, make an extraordinary impression.

▲ An Art Deco house still looks extraordinarily modern today; the latest furniture suits the interior just as well as reproductions of 1920s and 1930s classics.

◄ The striking façade of an Art Deco beach house modelled on those at Malibu, California. The large windows offer good views of the ocean and there is a generous sunroof.

▲ This apartment block is typical of those built in garden suburbs and some of the more prosperous parts of London in the early 1930s. For the hobbyist it would be a dream to complete internally, as each apartment could be decorated in an individual style and accessorized accordingly. The model consists of three flats plus a roof terrace.

▼ Distinctive, applied decoration was a feature of Art Deco buildings. On this British house, it is confined to a restrained motif over the bay window. The front entrance makes its own strong statement.

In Britain, surviving Art Deco houses are most commonly finished in white. With curving walls, balcony railings and the occasional porthole window, they lie in the landscape like ocean-going liners.

DECORATE IN THE ART DECO STYLE

In the late 1920s, new decoration schemes were initiated in the homes of fashionable society ladies who could afford to employ an interior decorator, and were taken up by others anxious to be in the forefront of home design. Syrie Maugham (the wife of Somerset Maugham) pioneered the idea of the all-white room when she had the music room of her Chelsea house decorated entirely in white; furnishings included white satin curtains and white velvet lampshades.

▲ The stunning interior of the dolls' house shown on page 47 has an elegant curving staircase with the typical balustrade of the period. This example is in 1/12 scale, but 1/24 house designs by the same maker are also available.

This was perhaps a little extreme but the idea filtered down to the less wealthy, and a scheme that is mostly in cream or beige with colour accents in green or vivid orange contrasted with glossy black will provide the essence of the Art Deco room. One much-copied fad of the time was 'Regency stripe' wallpaper, although this bore no relation to genuine Regency designs. I used giftwrap in white with a thin gold stripe to give the right effect.

▼ Simple and inexpensive materials can give a room the Art Deco look.

▲ This room leads off a hallway where a stained-glass window in the distinctive style of the period (cut from a magazine picture) looks spectacular. The floor is of slightly shiny cream card; fine wool would be equally suitable as a floor covering.

My reception room might have featured in an exclusive apartment in the early 1930s. It is designed to receive and impress visitors and there is a distinctly snobbish statement made by the cream flooring and sofa. It would be obvious to a visitor that such luxury could be kept pristine only with the attentions of a maid.

▲ Buttons and trimmings can be used as cushions or other decorative accessories.

▲ Wall lights are simulated by fancy buttons, and the electrified standard lamp is positioned behind the sofa to cast a gentle glow on the occupants. The painting (from a prints catalogue) is by Albert Gleizes, who had begun as an Impressionist painter but became a noted exponent of Cubism during the Art Deco period.

▶ A fancy silk-covered button represents a jewelled purse laid on the table.

TEXTURES

Textures are doubly important in a pale colour scheme. Try to add some sparkle: in my room I used a black mosaic glass mat to represent a small rug, and this produced the brittle effect I wanted to achieve. Shiny satin cushions show up well against the plain fabric-covered sofa.

For a low table, use a small, transparent plastic box; make the top of thick white card and cover it with leather-effect shiny plastic. In general, it is best to colour the edges of card to match a table top, but in this example the edge was left white deliberately to emphasize the contrast between shiny black, white and translucent 'glass'.

If space permits, a desirable addition to an Art Deco room could be a white baby grand piano, to give a Noel Coward effect. Inexpensive miniature pianos are widely available and a black one can be repainted with white, satin-finish model enamel.

OTHER ART DECO ESSENTIALS

A piece of sculpture, generally in the form of a stylized figure, was a much-admired ornament. Less expensive at the time but now extremely collectable, the bold and distinctive pottery of Clarice Cliff added colour and gaiety to even the most ordinary homes.

▶ This enchanting statuette is a copy of 'Con Brio', sculpted by Ferdinand Priess in 1935. It epitomizes the sense of movement that was so admired at the time. Priess was famed for his technical virtuosity and the miniaturist, in turn, has produced an exceptional figure, painted to resemble the original bronze and ivory.

▲▼ Clarice Cliff became the best-known designer of Art Deco pottery, and her patterns look equally well in miniature. Here (and on the facing page) is a selection of her instantly recognizable tableware, reproduced in porcelain in 1/12 by a talented miniaturist potter.

BATHROOMS

The Art Deco bathroom displayed as much originality as the rest of the house: the suite could be coloured, shapes were more streamlined and low baths were fitted with matching side panels.

THE ART DECO INFLUENCE

Despite being viewed initially with some reserve by the more traditionally inclined homeowner, the style influenced house design for many years to follow. In Britain especially, houses built during the 1930s often included details such as curved bays, porthole windows and sunray designs on garden gates.

In 2003, a mammoth Art Deco Exhibition at the Victoria and Albert Museum in London led to increased public interest. The style is appreciated by many dolls'

house hobbyists, and, as always, makers have responded to demand by producing furniture and accessories to complete both 1/12 and 1/24 dolls' houses.

▼ Black and white might be used in a bathroom, but as an alternative, a shade of green known as eau-de-Nil could be chosen. The shapes and detailing of this 1930s suite are characteristic of the period.

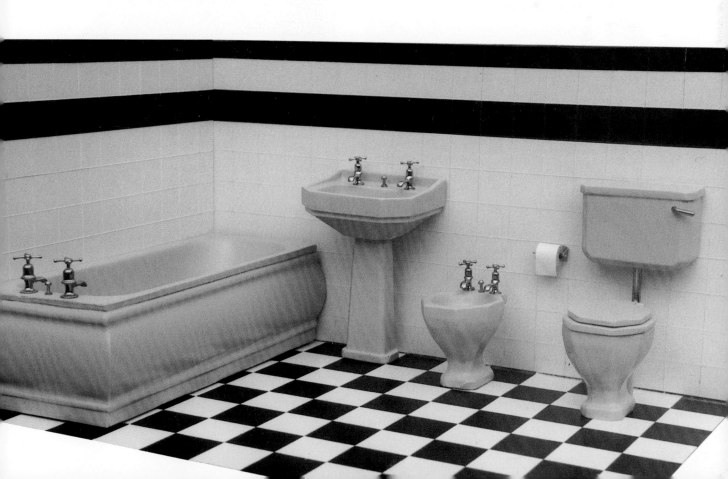

THE TRADITIONAL LOOK: 1920s AND 1930s

In the late 1920s and early 1930s, in contrast to the innovative Art Deco style, another type of house emerged – one that was to become known as 'Stockbroker Tudor'. Comfortable modern homes for the moderately wealthy took elements from the designs of Charles F.A. Voysey, the respected British architect who had incorporated vernacular features into his designs at the beginning of the twentieth century.

Such houses were built in leafy suburbs where the occupants could enjoy the advantages of country air. The houses were set well back from existing roads and given privacy and an air of exclusivity by tall boundary hedges and, typically, a 'spinney', a small wooded area beyond the formal gardens. Such a house was approached by a long, winding driveway so that, in the manner of a stately home, the building was revealed only after entering the formal garden.

▲ A beautiful porch and front door that derive directly from Voysey's style.

▼ 'Fairbanks' is a fine example of the Stockbroker Tudor genre, with six rooms and both front and side openings. This large dolls' house measures 33¾in (860mm) wide, 27½in (700mm) deep and 28¾in (730mm) high, and also has a garden area. It is available fully finished or as a kit, and is supplied with a turntable.

◀ A house assembled from a kit can be customized to suit your own inclinations, provided you have the necessary skills. This adaptation from a 'Fairbanks' kit was built by a hobbyist who enjoys the hands-on approach.

These houses were finished to a high standard internally, with solid oak-panelled doors and staircases, a legacy of the Arts and Crafts Movement.

▼ The inside of 'Fairbanks' is as detailed as the façade. Stained glass in the top lights of the windows and the front door, with its impressive surround, all add colour, while the deep window sills allow for further miniatures to be arranged to complement the adjacent rooms.

▲ A stone birdbath was a much-liked garden ornament during the 1930s.

THE KITCHEN

A 1930s kitchen is now a real period piece. Gas cookers were already in general use; electric cookers had just arrived on the scene but were considered expensive to run and somewhat alarming. A refrigerator was a new luxury that gradually replaced the old-fashioned larder.

▶ A 1930s kitchen cabinet with a central fold-down shelf that could be closed up when not in use. These were surprisingly capacious – dry goods such as sugar and tea were kept in the lower cupboards and everyday china at the top. Pale green was the standard colour: this looked attractive against cream walls and a red quarry-tiled floor.

▼ In most middle-class homes, a 'daily' woman and a gardener-cum-handyman, who came in once or twice a week, were employed to help with the chores. The cleaning woman in this kitchen is working at an old-fashioned Belfast sink, and it is interesting that these are again considered desirable in expensively finished twenty-first-century kitchens.

◀ The latest labour-saving device for dealing with the weekly wash was an electric washing machine with an integral hand wringer. This was a great improvement on the old-fashioned tub, rubbing-board and a heavy mangle, all kept outside in a yard at the back of the house. The machine was filled from a hose attached to the kitchen tap – and note the tap at the bottom to empty it. The machine needed constant attention during the wash period.

SUBURBAN HOUSING

Charles Voysey would have been amazed to see the miles of ribbon development of 'mock-Tudor' houses that adapted his country house ideas to the smaller home during the 1930s. Such houses were in great demand: they looked back to the past but had neat, well-designed interiors and were not too expensive for the average family. In 1936 the price of a basic semi-detached house was less than £1000.

The semi-detached house always had three bedrooms, although the third was very small, often referred to in the estate agent's particulars as a box room but more often used as a child's bedroom. Kitchens and bathrooms were half-tiled, and French

▲ The 1930s child was well provided with toys. For small boys, a pedal car, preferably red, was the favourite to race around the garden. For little girls, a Triang dolls' house could be played with for hours.

windows from the dining room led to the back garden, with a paved area next to the house. There was a small front garden for show, but the back provided a private space to sit out, garden or play games.

◄ This model is a superior house with a generous quarry-tiled porch, topped by brick facing, again following Voysey's lead. The windows on either side of the front door let plenty of light into the hall, which would have had a parquet floor, or, at the least, oak planks. The front gate is in the Art Deco sunray pattern. This dolls' house can be obtained in 1/12 or 1/24 and kits or plans are available for the 1/12 version.

MAKE A TERRACE

It is easy to add a terrace extension to the wall of a suburban-style house; some homes will already have a wall that extends to form the side wall of a terrace, but, if not, one can be fixed in place. The terrace can be of any size to suit your dolls' house.

This terrace measures 12in (305mm) long by 7½in (190mm) wide and is fitted against one wall of a brick-finished house. The added side wall is of wood, 12in (305mm) long by 9in (230mm) high, covered with textured white card.

▶ A popular garden ornament was a brightly painted gnome. Some gardens became overrun with them, while others had just one or two peeping shyly from behind shrubs. They are great fun in a miniature garden. These two cheery little fellows are of pewter, which you can paint for yourself.

▼ Tintin and Snowy, whose adventures began in 1929, are spending a lazy afternoon before setting off on a new expedition. Transport awaits on the brick parking space.

◄ White flowers snipped from a larger spray of plastic flowers are placed in a neatly edged border; they show up well against the brick wall.

Owners of suburban houses in the 1920s and 1930s favoured straight, neat borders. Edge the borders with stripwood or narrow brass trim. Make a slightly raised border of simulated earth or gravel, so that flowers or shrubs can be fixed in easily.

INTERIOR DECORATION

Decoration and furnishing of the average home followed traditional styles rather than Art Deco, although Clarice Cliff pottery, or ceramic flying ducks on the walls, can be included. Walls should be painted in plain colours: cream was most commonly chosen downstairs, while pink was favoured for bedrooms. Paintwork was generally cream, although there was a short-lived fashion for wood-graining.

▼ The 1930s lounge (the new buzzword which replaced sitting room in the suburban home) was designed for comfort. The three-piece suite or sofa and two matching armchairs appears inviting as afternoon tea is about to be served.

THE DINING ROOM

Reproduction Tudor or Jacobean furniture was favoured for dining rooms, so Tudor-style dolls' house furniture is appropriate. The average dining room had a dark oak dresser or an 'Elizabethan' court cupboard, a gateleg table that could be opened out when needed, ladderback chairs with leather or rush seats, and pewter ornaments.

Tudor-style wall lights were simulated by antique-finish metal wall brackets and shades made of parchment placed over candle-shaped bulbs. To harmonize with this period look, a model of an Elizabethan galleon completed the scheme.

▲ The red-brick fireplace (ready-made) is cosier than a tiled one, and gives an impression of the much-admired Tudor look. The china 'crinoline lady' figure on the mantelshelf featured in many homes. The up-to-date electric fire saved a lot of work in laying and lighting a traditional coal fire, as well as clearing up the resultant ash and dust.

Furnishings were standardized in the 1930s home. As well as the matching three-piece suite, you can include a period 'wireless', a standard or table lamp and a small bookcase. Plain fitted carpet (use woollen dress fabric) or a patterned carpet square centred on a stained wood surround are both suitable.

▶ One or two cane-topped low stools were often present in the 1930s lounge. They could be used either as footstools or as extra seating for children. There were several different designs of woven top: here are two, made by hand using linen thread with meticulous attention to detail.

▲ A dining table with extending leaves and a set of Yorkshire-style ladderback chairs, which includes two carvers, would add distinction to a dolls' house dining room.

In the bedroom there should be a freestanding wardrobe and a dressing table. The dressing table was fitted with a mirror with two additional side sections, and a low stool with an upholstered top was always provided so that make-up and hair styling could be attended to in comfort.

▶ Bedrooms were still cold, so a warm eiderdown or quilt was essential. This hand-embroidered silk quilt features the well-known crinoline lady design, which also appeared on crockery, trays and tablecloths throughout the 1930s. Transfers could be bought, and many ladies enjoyed embroidery as a hobby. Before the Second World War, a housewife's place was firmly in the home, and embroidery was an absorbing pastime.

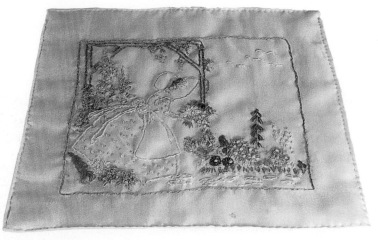

TEATIME

Afternoon tea was still a fixture: in the words of a popular song of the time, 'Everything Stops For Tea'. Brought in from the kitchen on a tea trolley and served in the lounge, this typically consisted of buttered scones with jam or honey and small fancy cakes.

The teapot was covered with a tea cosy to keep the brew warm. It is interesting that nowadays we seem to have hot tea without this accessory. However, if you plan a teatime scene in a 1930s dolls' house you can make a tea cosy easily from a short length of bobble braid. Sew it into a circular shape with tiny stitches and gather the top ends together to fit around and over the teapot.

▼ A 1930s-style tearoom in 1/24, serving home-made cakes in an unsophisticated setting. It is based on surviving examples, which both locals and visiting tourists love.

▲ A mahogany tea trolley fitted with brass castors, complete with beehive-shaped honey pot and a teapot with the obligatory tea cosy.

A 1930s TEAROOM

Teatime vanished from the home scene with the onset in 1939 of the Second World War, but the 1930s high street tearoom, where ladies met for a gossip and refreshment, continued in use and remains virtually unchanged in many British towns and villages today.

MAKE A TEAROOM

A tearoom is an enjoyable project that can be set in a room box. Use a pretty wallpaper and a patterned carpet, and add bought or home-made furniture. Such places usually have lots of pictures on the walls and a scattering of ornaments to interest the customers.

MAKE ROUND TABLES WITH CLOTHS

To provide a number of tables in your tearoom, one economical method is to make round tables from empty cotton reels topped with thick card.

1 Draw round a suitably sized jar lid as a pattern for the card tops. Cover with circular, floor-length tablecloths made from fine cotton.

2 To make a pattern to cut the floor-length tablecloth that will hide the cotton reel base, draw round a saucer or tea plate to mark the size and try it out in tissue paper first to make sure that the measurement is just right. It is surprising how large such a circular cloth needs to be to cover well. Damp the cloth, fit on the table, and use masking tape to hold it in place until

the folds have dried without sticking out too far.

3 Add teatime food, pretty china and a vase or two of flowers to complete the scene.

◀ A 1/12 porcelain tea set in Blue Roses, a typical pattern and shape from the 1930s.

▶ Small pewter objects are popular as gifts. This fancy box, complete with a tea service on the lid, is exactly right for a 1/24 room. Painted with model enamel, using a fine brush, even the tablecloth looks realistic.

THE WARTIME YEARS: 1940s

The average home interior remained unchanged during the 1940s due to the scarcity of materials during the Second World War, and for several years thereafter. In any case, people had other priorities than home decoration.

But the miniatures hobby encompasses memories as well as period and modern design, and hobbyists whose families lived through the war often relish the challenge of recreating their home and some of the atmosphere on the Home Front, which despite austerity was positive rather than depressing.

▼ You can build your own 'prefab' from plans and a photo pack together with a fittings kit, at a considerable saving on the price of a completed model. This option should appeal to many hobbyists who enjoy assembling or building a dolls' house model, and who have memories of living in such a home, often long after the war.

PREFABRICATED HOUSES

House building in Europe during the late 1940s was confined to replacing the housing stock that had been destroyed, whereas in America modern designs continued to increase. Prefabrication was the answer to

▲ The essentials of wartime on the Home Front: a gas mask in its standard cardboard case, which had to be carried at all times even by the youngest schoolchild, an identity card and a ration book were all part and parcel of everyday life.

▲ The prefab interior was neat and well laid out. One of the design stipulations was that the hallway should be wide enough to accommodate a perambulator, with enough space left to walk past it easily. Here is an inside view: the prefab is fully lit, decorated in the paint colours used at the time, and complete with simulated linoleum, a hard-wearing floor covering.

the British housing crisis, following a suggestion by Prime Minister Winston Churchill, and assembly started in earnest in 1945.

Originally, the prefabricated houses were intended to last for no more than ten years, but people found them snug and convenient and they needed little upkeep. When they were finally phased out, in some cases not until thirty-five years later, many older people who had lived in them since the 1940s were sad to leave.

DIG FOR VICTORY

Patriotic Britons dug up their flower gardens to grow vegetables to supplement their meagre diet. Food shortages and rationing of some foods continued even until the early 1950s, and digging, planting and harvesting crops replaced mowing the lawn as a weekend and evening activity.

▼ Vegetables freshly dug from the soil and a handy spade are appropriate for the wartime garden.

Keen miniaturists furnishing a prefab or a house in wartime style might like to reproduce a small garden, too. Vegetables planted in neat rows always look attractive. One easy way to miniaturize a vegetable plot is to use corrugated cardboard as a base. Choose a suitable size to reproduce the rows for the vegetables and paint the card a dull brown.

When dry, spread over with glue and cover with 'earth' using fine tea or coffee grounds. When the glue is dry, turn the card upside down to shake off the surplus and repeat the process to cover any bare patches. Add cabbages, lettuces or whatever you fancy.

▼ An evocative re-creation of a VE Day Party to celebrate the end of the war in Europe. Things could only get better from then on – although it took quite a few years before life returned to normal.

▲ People were encouraged to grow their own vegetables and cook them using economical and nourishing recipes, provided in a series of pamphlets issued by the government.

THE 1950s

In the 1950s new decorative schemes were limited initially by the scarcity of fabrics, furniture and all the accessories that we take for granted today. People longed for bright colours and patterns after all the years of 'make do and mend'.

A FRESH START

A surge of optimism and new ideas was inspired by the Festival of Britain in 1951, promoting innovative styles for the second half of the twentieth century. Magazines such as *Ideal Home* showed how to create the new look.

DECORATIONS AND FABRICS

Fabrics in vivid colours enlivened the 1950s room. Walls were decorated in contrasting styles, with just one wall papered and the others plainly painted. Another new idea for wall covering was to use hessian – a rich tan colour was a popular shade – which also had the advantage of deadening sound. This, too, was generally used on a single wall or on a cupboard front.

On a dolls' house wall, use linen or linen-look fabric to suggest the texture. Make a card template and glue the fabric on to that before fixing it to the wall with double-sided Scotch tape.

Patterned carpets featured geometric shapes rather than the unimaginative florals used in the typical pre-war home. It is worth checking out the table linen department of your local store to find place mats that can be used to simulate floor coverings. You should find a good selection of designs, including linen, plastic, printed, embroidered or woven, with many colours and patterns to choose from. Most are sold singly, so the cost of carpeting an entire dolls' house will be minimal.

▼ This room is arranged for a pleasant evening listening to the long-playing vinyl records that preceded compact discs, and its decorations are very up to date for the time. The pictured curtain fabric, used here as wallpaper, is 'Calyx', designed by Lucienne Day in 1951. The chairs, made from mobile phone holders with a retro 'look', are based on a design that would have been at the height of modernity during the 1950s.

MAKE A RECORD PLAYER

To make a record player that is suitable for the 1950s room you need a small flat box, large enough to take a turntable on which to fit miniature records: these are available in packs complete with copies of old record sleeves.

1 A box about 1⅛in (30mm) square and ½in (13mm) deep will be suitable, either black or in a dark colour.

2 Fit a square of ¼in (6mm) thick black card into the box as a base and add a washer, also painted black, to simulate the turntable.

3 To make the arm to take the gramophone needle, bend a small piece of metal into a curve and glue it into the corner of the box so it is poised above the record. Almost any small piece of metal can be used – part of a paper clip, a short nail that can be bent into shape with pliers or, my choice, part of the metal clip from the back of an old brooch.

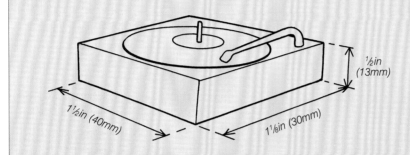

½in
(13mm)

1½in (40mm)

1⅛in (30mm)

FURNITURE

Teak was the most widely used wood for the new furniture, supplanting oak and mahogany. Scandinavian design had a strong influence: shallow cupboards were fitted with sliding doors and plain sofas were perched on thin, straight legs.

A coffee table became the focus of many sitting rooms. This was a relatively new piece of furniture, to cater for an increase in coffee drinking and the prevalence of low seating. For young people, the coffee bar rather than the pub (public house) was at the heart of the new social scene outside the home in the 1950s.

◄ The overriding impression left by furniture designed in the 1950s is of straight, spiky legs. Here are two typical tables, one with a glass top that allows an interesting view of the cross-braces below. The other has a marble top, but Formica, a new wipe-clean material that could be patterned to resemble marble, was preferred to the real thing at the time, and was much cheaper.

▲ Swedish glass and stylish ceramic ornaments accessorized the plain teak furniture. These handkerchief vases are made in porcelain.

MAKE A COFFEE TABLE

A replica Formica-topped coffee table is simple to provide:

1 For the base, use a small box approximately ¾in (20mm) tall, 2in (50mm) long and 1½in (40mm) wide and paint it black.

2 Cut stiff ¼in (6mm) thick card to make the table top, 2½in (65mm) long by 1½in (40mm) wide. Cover with a suitably patterned, shiny card to simulate Formica. Colour the edges of the table top to match or tone with the 'Formica' pattern.

3 Glue the top to the base.

The measurements of the coffee table can be adapted to suit the size of your room.

FURNITURE FOR THE BEDROOM
Built-in bedroom furniture began to replace free-standing pieces. One novelty of the time was an extended headboard that linked cupboards on either side of the bed without taking up floor space.

▶ The bedhead and bedside cupboards could be painted to suit the colour scheme. The wardrobe shown resembles the popular G-Plan furniture that superseded wartime basic utility furniture. Although still plainly styled, the quality was generally excellent.

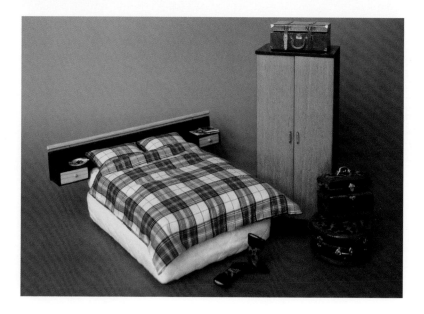

A NEW COLOUR FOR THE NURSERY

Traditional nurseries were still popular, and the furniture was decorated with rabbits, ducks or teddy bears. With the introduction of so many new ideas on home decoration, the nursery was not entirely left out: yellow and white as an alternative colour scheme to the prevailing pink for a girl or blue for a boy was introduced in the late 1950s and at first was considered quite daring. This did have the

▼ The yellow and white colour scheme is fresh and appealing, and the candy-stripe wallpaper is exactly right for the 1950s. The nursery furniture is hand-painted in a Noah's Ark design and the frieze at child's eyelevel continues this theme. The play furniture (by a different maker) is also hand-painted and is designed in a size to suit the 1/12 child doll.

▲ The artist-maker who decorated the nursery furniture also produced this delightful oil painting to add a colourful note to the room.

clear-cut advantage that the nursery could be decorated and ready before the gender of the baby was known: by the 1950s many parents did their own decorating and were not as quick as professional decorators.

Accessorize the nursery just as you would for a real baby or toddler. Bear in mind that wooden toys suit the period better than today's plastic.

▶ Packaging that is strong enough to be used, a small blackboard complete with chalked figures and a drawing, and a tiny painted dolls' house will all add interest to the 1/12 nursery.

◀ A nursery will look its best with the addition of some child dolls. This adorable little toddler is by a French maker.

THE MODERNIST HOUSE IN THE TWENTIETH CENTURY

The first modernist houses in the 1920s and 1930s were greeted with astonishment. They were built for wealthy clients by architects such as Le Corbusier and Mies van der Rohe. In Britain, the majority of people preferred traditional homes to gleaming white walls and expanses of glass. These seemed to provide little privacy for the occupants, even though many such houses were raised up on columns or pillars.

In Britain, the preferred home for the wealthy in the early twentieth century was a centuries-old manor house. Modern designs were accepted more readily in Spain and in California, where the climate is better and where these minimalist structures seemed to suit the landscape.

By the 1950s, the priority in Britain was to provide inexpensive housing to replace that which had been destroyed in the Second World War; architects were designing concrete blocks of flats rather than innovative one-off designs. In America it was a different story. Some beautiful homes were built in the 1950s; ground space was not at a premium and many were spacious one- or two-storey houses incorporating glass, brick, concrete and steel to provide light-filled rooms.

▲A 1/24 scale dolls' house adapted from the Farnsworth House by Mies van der Rohe, designed in the 1950s.

▼A 1/12 scale dolls' house adapted from a house built by Philip Johnson in the 1950s.

MAKE YOUR OWN MODERNIST HOUSE

A modernist house is the perfect display unit for the dolls' house hobbyist who enjoys modern furniture. Collecting and minimalism may seem contradictory but it is rewarding to make your own modernist house and create a perfect setting for a few well-chosen pieces.

I have chosen two iconic designs to miniaturize: both built in America in the mid-twentieth century. They were considered so special that they have recently been renovated, and are still admired by architects throughout the world today. Houses derived from these designs can now be seen in Britain, although it has taken until the twenty-first century for minimalism finally to become accepted.

These houses are easy to make – particularly if foamboard is used rather than the more difficult-to-cut plywood as the main component (see Practical Matters, page 11, for details of foamboard). I hope you will enjoy choosing and making one of these designs.

▲ The completed miniature of the Farnsworth House.

DESIGN 1: 1/24 scale house

To begin, here is a small-scale model. The completed house measures 23in (585mm) long by 7in (180mm) deep by 7½in (190mm) high. The Farnsworth House was designed and built by Mies van der Rohe in Illinois during 1945–1951, restored twenty-three years later, and again renovated during 1997–1998.

Le Corbusier began the trend for the all-white house, but Mies van der Rohe went one stage further with the amount of glass he used in his 'see-through' houses, of which Farnsworth is, perhaps, the most famous example. The effect of weightlessness and light is enchanting.

This dolls' house is an almost transparent, elongated pavilion with an open front. No electric lighting is necessary, as the effect of the model displayed in a well-lit room is magical. It is made of foamboard, acetate sheet, semi-transparent envelope stiffener and wood dowel. (See Practical Matters, pages 10–12, for where to obtain these materials, plus information on cutting and glueing.)

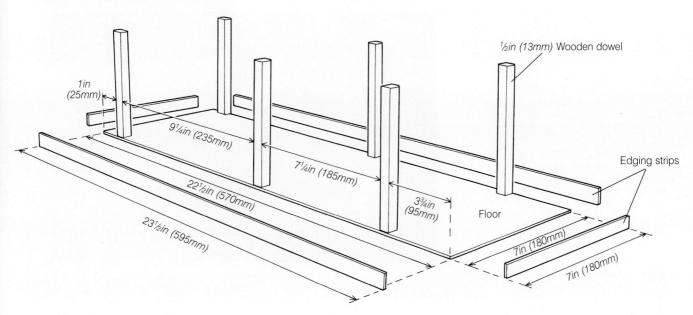

1in (25mm)

9¼in (235mm)

½in (13mm) Wooden dowel

7¼in (185mm)

22½in (570mm)

3¾in (95mm)

Floor

Edging strips

23½in (595mm)

7in (180mm)

7in (180mm)

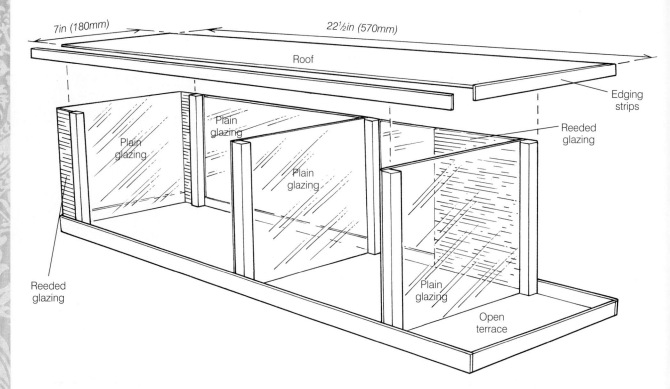

7in (180mm)   22½in (570mm)

Roof

Edging strips

Plain glazing

Plain glazing

Reeded glazing

Plain glazing

Plain glazing

Reeded glazing

Plain glazing

Open terrace

1 Cut one piece of foamboard 22½in (570mm) L x 7in (180mm) W for the floor. To edge the floor, cut two strips of foamboard 23in (585mm) L x ¾in (20mm) W, and two strips 7in (180mm) L x ¾in (20mm) W.

2 Glue the edging strips to the floor in the sequence shown, with the lower edges level with the base of the floor.

3 Cut six pieces of dowel, each 7in (180mm) L, and paint white. If preferred, the wood can be painted before cutting, as the cut ends will not need painting.

a) Measure and mark the positions for the wooden pillars as shown. This will give one large room and one smaller room, plus a terrace extending a further 3¾in (95mm) beyond the pillars at one end.

b) Glue the pillars to the base and inside of the edging strips, making

sure that the pillars at the back are exactly opposite to those at the front.

4 Cut and fit the glazing to represent glass walls. A mixture of plain and reeded will enhance the effect.

a) Cut two pieces reeded, both 7in (180mm) H x 1in (25mm) W to fit left-hand end spaces, and two pieces plain, both 7in (180mm) H x 7in (180mm) W for each end of

the house. Glue the 1in (25mm) wide strips of glazing to the pillars at the left-hand end, then glue the 1in x 7in (25mm x 180mm) W piece to the glazing strips and to the floor and inside of the edging strips.

b) Glue the second piece of 7in (180mm) W glazing at the right-hand end of the house *inside* the pillars. This will leave an open terrace beyond.

▲ This shows how the glazing is fitted to the walls.

c) To glaze the back of the house, cut one piece of plain glazing 13½in (345mm) L x 6½in (165mm) H and one piece of reeded glazing 7in (180mm) H x 4½in (115mm) W. Glue the plain glazing on top of the base edging at the back of the house and to the pillars. Then glue the 4½in (115mm) W piece of reeded glazing to overlap on the inside to give the impression of a sliding door.

d) Cut one piece of plain glazing 7in (180mm) H x 7in (180mm) W. Glue to left-hand side of the off-centre pillars to form the room divider.

5 Cut one piece of foamboard measuring 22½in (570mm) L x 7in (180mm) W for the roof.

To edge the roof, cut two strips of foamboard 23in (585mm) L x ½in (13mm) W.

Glue the edging strips to the roof as shown, then glue the completed roof in place to the tops of the pillars and glazing.

The house should appear to float above the ground rather than rest on it. I substituted a plinth for the pillars that raised the real house above the ground, as I felt they would be vulnerable to accidental damage in such a small scale. The plinth base gives a similar feeling.

For the plinth, use a block of wood approximately 8in (205mm) L x 5½in (140mm) W x 2in (50mm) H, centred under the house. This will not show around the edges and gives the desired effect of a light, almost floating structure. If you do not have a suitable piece of wood, use a box of similar dimensions (with a weight inside) to stabilize the house.

FURNISHING THE HOUSE

Furniture needs to be carefully chosen to give the best effect, and the architect obviously didn't consider that his clients might want to hang pictures, although it would be possible to display a painting on an easel. Ceramic objects or small sculptures are shown to advantage.

In my model I decided to emphasize the sparkling crystal effect with clear, plastic furniture glass accessories, and only a hint of colour. Ready-made 1/24 furniture would also look well, either special craftsman-made pieces or inexpensive furniture that you can paint in the colour of your choice.

▲ The terrace extension with just one pot plant and glass exterior 'lights'. The string of lights by the sliding door entrance is a thin wire bracelet, strung with blue glass beads. The miniature birds are of hand-blown glass.

▼ Floating in air! The almost transparent house appears weightless. Blue glass mosaic coasters used as tiled areas and plastic furniture and glass accessories are delicate and add sparkle.

DESIGN 2: 1/12 scale house

My second choice is based on a home in Connecticut, designed and built during 1955–1956 by architect Philip Johnson and restored in 1998.

This house is modern in style but not aggressively so: it follows the lead of American Frank Lloyd Wright and, in England, Edwin Lutyens, who both designed homes that included traditional elements and liked to use materials such as brick, stone and wood. This house was designed for a wealthy client, and set in a green space rather than hemmed in by other homes.

It has space, light and the warmth of brick, and will appeal to the hobbyist who wants to include furniture of any period from the 1950s to the present. The idea is to bring the outside indoors; wood cladding is used on some walls, while pale floors provide an airy, spacious feeling.

The dolls' house version is open-fronted, making it easily accessible, and with no door frames or hinges to fit, it is straightforward to make. Both pictures and diagrams are provided for reference as you work. The completed house, including the small base extension, measures 31in (790mm) L x 14in (355mm) D x 12in (300mm) H.

◄ The completed house: downlighters on the façade, provided on the original building, are simulated here by square, gilt buttons.

MATERIALS

Two A0 size sheets of 5mm (approx. ⅕in) foamboard.

Seven 36in (915mm) lengths of ½in (13mm) wide stripwood (to paint black for roof trim and window frames).

Two large sheets of dolls' house brick paper.

(Note: when buying brick paper, select a good-quality one with a matt finish; cheaper versions are too shiny, do not look realistic and will easily tear.)

One sheet of cream artists' mounting board to fit as a floor (or an alternative colour if preferred).

Two pieces of acetate sheet for glazing, each 9in (230mm) W x 11in (280mm) H.

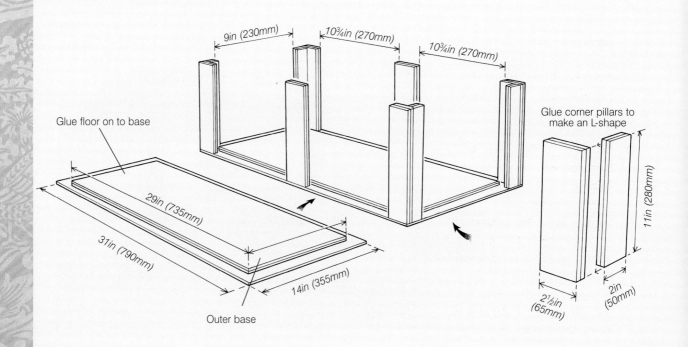

9in (230mm) 10¾in (270mm) 10¾in (270mm)

Glue corner pillars to make an L-shape

Glue floor on to base

29in (735mm)

31in (790mm)

14in (355mm)

Outer base

11in (280mm)

2½in (65mm) 2in (50mm)

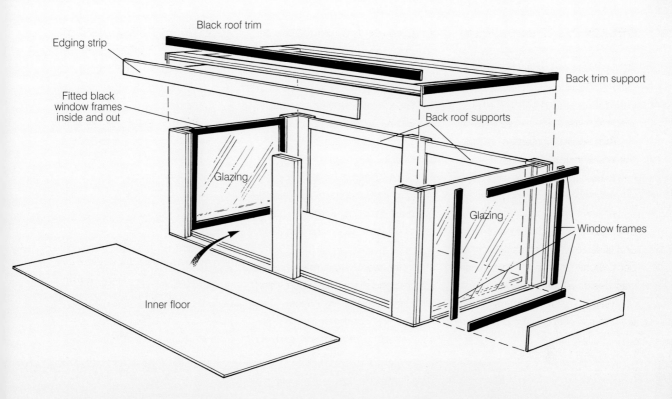

Black roof trim

Edging strip

Fitted black
window frames
inside and out

Glazing

Inner floor

Back trim support

Back roof supports

Glazing

Window frames

1 Cut one piece of foamboard 31in (785mm) L x 14in (355mm) W for the base, then cut two pieces of foamboard, each measuring 29in (735mm) L x 12in (305mm) W to make a double-thickness floor. Glue together.

2 Centre the floor on the base and glue, leaving a 1in (25mm) extension all round. Cover the base extension with brick paper, folding and glueing the edges underneath the base; allow a 2in (50mm) overlap underneath.

3 Cut the supporting pillars from foamboard, which should be used double-thickness for strength.

a) Cut four pieces 11in (280mm) H x 2½in (65mm) W for the centre pillars. Glue two pieces together to make each pillar.

b) Cut eight pieces 11in (280mm) H x 2½in (65mm) W and eight pieces

11in (280mm) H x 2in (50mm) W for the corner pillars. Glue two pieces together to make double-thickness foamboard of each width.

c) To assemble each corner pillar, glue 1 x 2½in (65mm) width to 1 x 2in (50mm) width to make an L-shape for each corner.

4 Cover each of the pillars with brick paper, glueing in place with a neat join at the inner corner of the

L-shape, and along one inner edge of the two flat centre pillars.

a) Glue corner pillars to each corner of the floor and to the base extension.

b) Glue flat pillars, to create a central division for two room spaces, to the edge of the floor and to the base extension. Equally spaced, each room will be 10¾in (275mm) L.

▼ Work in progress!

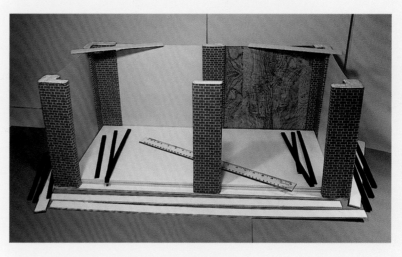

5 Cut two pieces of art mounting board, each 10¾in (275mm) L x 11in (280mm) H to make back walls. Paint or paper the walls.

a) Mark a vertical line down the centre of each side of the back pillars and glue the walls in place, leaving an equal amount of brick showing on both the outside and inside of the house.

b) Cut two strips of foamboard each 1in (25mm) W x 10¾in (275mm) L. Glue along top of back walls between pillars inside the house.

6 The side walls are glazed with rigid acetate sheet.

a) Cut two pieces, both approx. 9in (230mm) W x 11in (280mm) H. Check the space between the pillars for any slight variation in the structure before you cut the glazing, so that it fits exactly.

b) Glue the glazing in place down the centre of each pillar, taking care not to smear glue on to the glazing. (See Practical Matters, pages 11–12, for advice on glueing.)

7 Fit the inner floor using mount board, or any surface of your choice.

8 Cut eight pieces of ½in (13mm) stripwood (painted black), each 9in (230mm) L, and eight pieces 10½in (265mm) L to make the inner and outer window frames. Attach with double-sided Scotch tape. Fit the base strips first, then side and top strips. Before fitting, check each measurement and trim length if necessary.

▼ The rear living-room wall is coloured plain cream to take a card reproduction of a large painting of trees. The effect is, as the architect intended, to bring the outside indoors and visually link the interior with the surrounding woodland.

a)   After fitting the exterior window frames, cut two pieces of foamboard 9in (230mm) L x 1½in (38mm) W and cover with brick paper, joining at one edge. Fit at the base of each window, outside between pillars.

9   Cut one piece of foamboard 30in (760mm) L x 13in (330mm) W for the roof. Check the measurements before cutting the roof to allow for any slight variation. It should cover the tops of the pillars exactly. Glue on top of pillars, back walls and side glazing.

a)   Cut two pieces of foamboard each 30½in (775mm) L x 1½in (40mm) W and two pieces 13in (330mm) L x 1½in (40mm) W for front and side roof edging. Glue side edging to pillars and edge of roof. Glue front and back edging, to cover the ends of the side edging.

10 Cut two strips of foamboard each measuring 29½in (750mm) L x 1in (25mm) wide and two strips 9in (230mm) L x 1in (25mm) wide. These will act as supports for the roof trim.

a)   For the roof trim, cut two pieces of black-painted ½in (13mm) woodstrip, each 30in (760mm) L, and two pieces each 13½in (345mm) L. Glue the black trim to the top of the white roof edging. Glue the side pieces first, then front and back to cover the side edges of the roof trim.

b)   Glue the 1in (25mm) wide foamboard strips flat to the top of the roof and to the black trim. These will act as a support. Check measurements and trim to fit exactly if necessary before glueing.

THE OPEN-PLAN INTERIOR

There are two 3in (75mm) wide wooden walls fitted against the central pillars to make partial room dividers without spoiling the open-plan effect. The 3in (75mm) wide rear divider screens off the stove from the bedroom, and can be covered with brick paper before fitting. You can buy a ready-made stove, but for economy and a splash of colour I used a red tape dispenser standing on its end, and added logs to provide a realistic touch.

This house is intended primarily as a display unit for miniature furniture and does not have a separate kitchen. If you want to include a kitchen area, the space can be subdivided by adding an extra room divider where you wish. Similarly, an en suite shower could be fitted into a corner of the bedroom.

Colour coordination is important in an open-plan house. Cream and taupe contrast well with brick and wood-grain walls, and rugs in each room are rust-coloured. Keep to a few basic soft shades and then add furniture in a brighter colour so that it shows up well, such as the sofas featuring a deep, bright blue. The black Wassily chair in the living room was designed by Marcel Breuer in 1925 and is still manufactured today. The seating furniture is from an inexpensive range from a mail order supplier.

USE FURNITURE THAT IS IN KEEPING WITH THE HOUSE

Furniture designed in the 1950s, when the real house was first built, would create a striking effect in the large rooms.

To supplement bought furniture, make some modern pieces of your own; the colour or finish can be adapted to suit your scheme.

▶ The sculptural-looking Egg chair was designed by Arne Jacobsen during 1957–1958, with a moulded fibreglass seat shell that, in the original, swivels on a cast aluminium base. His intention was to keep the chair lightweight, and with this construction only a minimum of padding was needed. They were not especially comfortable but still look modern today.

◀ The log-burning stove gives a comfortable feeling to the living room. The room divider at the front of the house is covered with wood-effect paper to match the back wall of the bedroom.

▲ The bedroom is spacious enough to take a sofa as well as the bed. The duvet is a lavender bag, which also adds fragrance to the room, and is covered in taupe linen, while the bedside tables are small boxes with an interesting texture. The back wall is covered with wood-effect paper, which continues the theme of the woodland pictured on the living-room wall.

◀ The Tulip table and chair were designed by Eero Saarinen during 1955–1956. His avowed purpose in designing single pedestal supports was to clear up the mess of legs in domestic interiors – and he succeeded brilliantly. These miniature versions are in 1/12.

MAKE A BED

You will need a plain box approximately 7in (180mm) L x 4in (100mm) W to form the bed base.

1 Make the headboard from ¼in (6mm) thick card, wood or foamboard. Pad the front of this with a piece of thin foam.

2 Cover with fabric, fold the edges over the headboard and foam and glue in place at the back.

3 Make a valance to match and fit around the bed base.

This is a house that was designed for twentieth-century modern living, but it remains equally suitable for the twenty-first century. Whether it is furnished with retro-1950s furniture or in the latest minimalist style, it will look attractive and comfortable. In either case, keep the furniture and accessories to a minimum to make the most of the spacious interior.

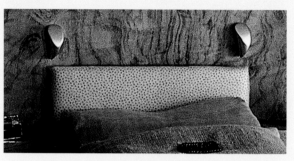

▲ A padded headboard is easy to make. The wall lights on either side of the bed are gilt buttons.

◀ The square table in the living room has a leather-effect top – a suitably textured art card – glued to a square box base. It is simple to make and effective.

Modern
Decorative Styles

Part 2

THE SWINGING SIXTIES

House building returned to pre-war levels during the 1960s, and those who could afford them employed architects to design spacious modern homes. Renovation of older houses was a popular alternative and this was seen especially in London, where so much of the existing housing stock was (and still is) Victorian.

To create more spacious rooms, it was common practice to 'knock through', which involved demolishing a non-structural dividing wall to make two small rooms into one large one. This was also a good way to reinvent a 1930s home, which invariably had a lounge and a separate dining room, and it spelled the beginning of the end for formal dining rooms.

THE DUAL-PURPOSE ROOM

There were two ways to create and use the new large room. One was to make the sitting and dining room into one, by placing a table and chairs at one end, and the other was to combine the sitting room and kitchen, sometimes with a low room divider between the two sections: eating in the kitchen soon became acceptable for dinner parties as well as for breakfast.

▲ Skips (dumpsters) became an everyday sight in the streets throughout the 1960s. This well-used-looking model would add that extra touch of realism outside a 1960s dolls' house.

▼ This 1/12 scale version of a large detached house built in the 1960s is made in three sections. The specially moulded 'stone cladding' reproduces the York stone used to build the real house.

This typical 1960s room is decorated in cheerful colours; the dining table is placed at one end. The room is accessorized with a new-style floor light with a glass shade and a tall metal stand, from an inexpensive range of dolls' house electric lighting.

MAKE A CURVED WALL

When a home was renovated, curved walls were sometimes introduced as part of the reorganisation. This is something that can be arranged in a dolls' house room to avoid a box-like effect. It looks attractive and a little unusual.

Art card is stiff enough to make a curved wall, and it has a suitably smooth surface. Select the right colour from the wide range available and there will be no need for further decoration.

1   Cut the card to the height of the room and long enough to cover the back wall and one side wall.

2   Glue it along most of the back wall, then curve the card around the corner and glue it again, firmly, to the front edge of the side wall.

3   Trim when the glue has set.

What you lose in reduced floor space, you will regain with an original and pleasing effect.

A bright modern rug on a darker carpet will enhance the colourful effect: photocopy a picture of a suitable rug and enlarge or reduce it to the size you need.

One wall in a colour contrast to the rest of the room emphasizes the separate eating area. Tile-topped tables became a feature: these could be wiped clean easily, with no need for a tablecloth that had to be laundered and then ironed. Ladderback chairs were enjoying a revival and reproductions could be bought from leading furniture stores.

Accessorize the 1960s room with pop art by well-known artists such as Andy Warhol and Roy Lichtenstein. Suitably sized reproductions can be cut from a prints catalogue or a magazine gallery guide.

RETRO STYLE

Another facet of 1960s decorations was retro style, which updated 1930s ideas. Instead of the all-white room, shades of lavender and grey with purple accents looked fresh and appealing, especially to those who enjoyed a more restrained and elegant decor.

▼Retro chic! This room is a blend of styles, all reproduced in the 1960s. The fireplace reinvents Art Deco style while the rug is a 1950s design and the striped sofa was thoroughly up to date for the time. The print over the fireplace is a copy of a painting by Yves Klein, who specialized in painting blocks of solid colour, particularly in a distinctive deep blue. A reproduction is easy to achieve in miniature size.

▲A slice of tree trunk was a clever idea for a coffee table. This miniature version is made from a wooden coaster, mounted on a small circular base – a cardboard tube from the centre of a roll of kitchen towels, painted dark grey. It had become acceptable to use mugs rather than cups and saucers, even when guests were present.

A PORTHOLE WINDOW

A porthole window is another period idea resurrected from the 1930s, but by the 1960s an oval shape looked newer and more interesting. Cutting out a perfect, small-size oval accurately is not easy. Solve this problem by using a card picture mount on one wall, with the shape already cut out. Fix a pictured view behind the 'window' before glueing the wall in place.

MAKE A SLATE-TOPPED COFFEE TABLE

To make the coffee table, all you need is a small slice of jagged natural slate – mine fell from the roof of my home. Failing this, use a slate coaster to make a round or square table top. Make a base, as for the 'tree trunk' coffee table; note that for a large table you may need to provide two supports.

FIREPLACES

With the increasing use of central heating during the 1960s, fireplaces were no longer considered essential: beautiful period designs were ripped out in their thousands, and the walls were replastered. Much too late, it was realized that a fireplace could be an important focal point even in a modern room, and during the 1980s and 1990s period fireplaces became sought after and reinstated. This was the start of architectural salvage as big business.

Modern fireplaces are straightforward to make, as they rely on plain shapes rather than elaborate mouldings. You can buy a ready-made fireplace in a choice of styles, but it is economical and also fun to make your own.

▲A room with a view: gentle colours harmonize in this room, while the slate coffee table provides a contrast in texture against the smooth surfaces of walls and floor.

◀The completed fireplace, accessorized with blue glass miniatures to accentuate the colour scheme of the room. This type of fireplace is suitable for any period since the 1930s and is easy to construct.

MAKE A FIREPLACE

This fireplace measures 5⅜in (135mm) L x 4in (100mm) H. The size can be adjusted to suit your room.

1 Cut a piece of ½in (13mm) thick balsa wood, 5⅜in (135mm) L x 4in (100mm) H. (Alternatively, you can use foamboard: you will need two layers glued together.)

2 Choose an art card in a colour to suit the room: I used a mottled grey.

CUT: one piece 5½in (140mm) L x 4in (100mm) H for the front of the fireplace

two pieces 4in (100mm) L x ½in (13mm) W for the sides

one piece 5½in (140mm) L x ½in (13mm) W for the top

one piece 5¾in (145mm) L x 2¼in (60mm) W for the hearth.

(Note: the card for the front and top are both fractionally longer than the balsa wood so that the side edges will be covered.)

3 Use part of a picture-mount oval as a pattern to cut the grate aperture. Centre it carefully and mark out the shape on the reverse of the card front, extending the lower edges slightly (see picture). Cut out the space.

4 Place the card over the balsa wood base and draw around the aperture. Cut out a space in the balsa slightly larger all round than the marked opening. Glue a piece of black card

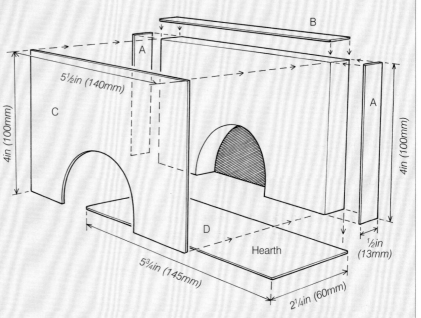

to the back of the fireplace to act as a fireback. Glue the coloured card to the fireplace in the sequence shown above.

5 Colour the edges of the hearth with a matching or toning felt-tip pen. Position the hearth and fix it to the floor with double-sided Scotch tape. Centre the fireplace on top and attach it to the wall and hearth with double-sided Scotch tape: this is preferable to glueing it permanently in position, in case you decide to change the room at a later date.

EXTEND THE HEARTH

Another new idea was to build a long platform and put the fireplace on top. You might like to consider this option before fitting a fireplace into a 1960s room.

1 You will need a piece of wood approximately ½in (13mm) thick, 1½in (40mm) wide and the length of the fireplace wall. Paint it white or a colour to suit your decorations.

2 Fit this against the wall and fix the fireplace centrally on top. The platform will provide a neat display space for books and ornaments, just as it did in a real 1960s home.

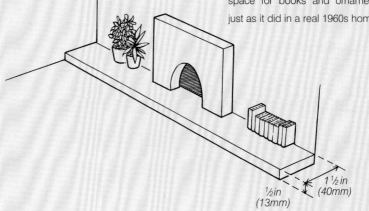

THE 1970s

A 1970s newbuild home made of concrete may not be very appealing when reproduced as a dolls' house. A common alternative was to update the interior of an older property, and you may prefer to arrange a home for the 1970s in a period dolls' house. Victorian houses, for example, are remarkably adaptable, and were frequently converted for twentieth-century family living.

COLOURFUL DECORATIONS

The colours used in the 1970s were often bright, even brash; purple and orange were both liked. Although the rooms might be startling, they suited the mood of a time when adventurous schemes were carried out and enjoyed. Geometrically patterned carpets or shagpile were both in fashion and added further interest.

FURNITURE

New furniture designs changed the appearance of the 1970s room, and the growing popularity of flat-pack furniture meant that homeowners could buy pieces more cheaply than in the past. One innovative concept was to have small cupboards and shelves screwed to

▲ A replica of a real home, a snug 1970s bungalow in 1/24, set on its own plot of land. Although small, this one-storey dwelling makes the most of the available interior space, as there is no staircase to work round. You could also enjoy planning the garden.

▼ An attractive conversion of a cottage and adjoining agricultural buildings to make a spacious family home, reproduced in 1/12. This type of conversion was very popular in the 1970s (as it is today) and rooms decorated in the latest style would be appropriate.

the wall rather than standing on legs. They appeared to float weightlessly and made the room space seem larger, a helpful effect in a miniature room, too.

A MORE TRADITIONAL LOOK

A calmer, more restful look also flourished to cater for conservative taste, and for this the favoured paint colour was the soft cream called 'magnolia'. This shade showed off furniture and accessories to advantage, and was above all safe for the less adventurous decorator – though eventually, so many interiors were painted magnolia that it became something of a joke.

Use cream to achieve this effect in a dolls' house, as true magnolia is a little dark in a small room. It would be suitable in a conventional bungalow like the one shown at the top of page 87.

▼ The flooring used in this room is giftwrap. Op Art rather than Pop Art was in vogue; striking prints based on spirals enliven the scene.

▼ The wall-hung bookcase is a card box, attached to the wall with double-sided Scotch tape. The miniature books are light in weight but if you want to display a heavier ornament, you will need to glue the box to the wall for additional security.

◀ Laminated cardboard furniture was another new development during the 1970s and was an instant success. This 'Wiggle' chair was designed by architect Frank O. Gehry in 1972, with the aim of making low-cost furniture, and a reproduction is now available in 1/12.

KITCHENS

The fitted kitchen had arrived, with plenty of cupboards and appliances that slid in under countertops. British kitchens were typically still rather small, and this arrangement made the most of the limited space. American kitchens, on the other hand, are nearly always more generously sized, but fitted kitchens were adopted there, too.

BEDROOMS

Bedrooms could be pretty and feminine or modern and colourful, according to taste. Both versions were considered fashionable.

▼A 1970s fitted kitchen with ample work surface above the storage cupboards. The wall cupboards have glass and mesh fronts so that the contents can be seen at a glance.

▲ A cottage-style window in this charming bedroom is emphasized by curtains with a pelmet. The dressing-table shelf with a triple mirror and a curtain to conceal a storage area underneath was considered suitable for a young girl.

◀ A more modern style for a sports-loving teenager contains furniture with contrasting coloured panels. The look is much bolder and gives a completely different effect. A check duvet with matching pillowcase is bright and cheerful.

THE BATHROOM

Bathroom design took a leap forward in the 1970s. The now old-fashioned plain bath was fitted with new side panels made of marble-patterned Formica. Bathrooms were often carpeted and sometimes even the bath side panels were covered with carpet to match.

This fashion was not a great success, as if water splashed over the side, the carpet got very wet and soon became stained. It is an option that can be adopted perhaps more successfully in a dolls' house bathroom.

▼ The status symbol for the 1970s bathroom was a corner bath with gold-plated taps. Avocado green was the most usual colour, but black was more striking. Fitted shagpile carpet often featured in the bathroom, too – you can make your own from a face flannel.

TEEN ROOMS

Most teenagers had a room of their own and were allowed to choose the decorations and some of the furniture. You might like to include one such room in a 1970s house or apartment, and if there are internal doors, a notice saying PRIVATE or KEEP OUT on the door would reflect the rebellious attitude of the time.

A record player or a radio was essential in a teen room. As yet, the only television set was in the main family living room but music was allowed, often played at top volume to the irritation of anyone else at home. 'Hi-fi' was in its infancy compared to today's sophisticated equipment, and the CD player was yet to come.

A rather old-fashioned-looking record player is appropriate, as it most likely would have been a hand-down from parents rather than newly bought. (See 1950s, page 66, for how to make a record player.) The posters of pop idols on the walls were cut from advertisements. An alternative way to display them is to provide a cork pin-up board: cut a slice from a thin cork tablemat to make one.

◄ A decorative wall plaque made from eight novelty buttons in the shape of bottle caps, with 'cola' printed on each. Mounted on a shiny red base, they might be recycled tops from the teenager's favourite drink.

▶ Shiny, black, plasticized paper makes a suitable floor for the teen room, while patterned giftwrap with a silver background and a brightly coloured design gives a disco effect to the back wall.

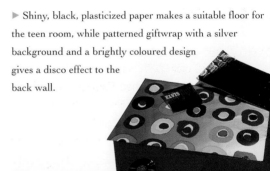

▼ A lively room, with the type of decorations chosen by the 1970s teenager, is arranged ready for a party. Saturday night was party night in the 1970s and cola was the favourite drink. If possible, the parents would arrange to be out that evening.

MAKE A RECORDING STUDIO

A visit to a recording studio was a teenager's idea of heaven in the 1970s. If you enjoy pop music, you might like to make a small studio in a room box. Mine was inspired by finding the striking black patterned giftwrap to use on the walls and the iridescent plasticized sheet, which was easy to cut with scissors, to fit as a floor.

There are always lots of cables trailing around when music is being recorded, and these can be simulated with black cord. Add inexpensive musical instruments as you wish: a keyboard is particularly useful for this setting. To simulate loudspeakers for either a teen room or a recording studio, use two small blocks of wood of a suitable size and paint them a matt black.

▼A recording studio with plenty of atmosphere.

THE 1980s

In the 1980s, the traditional country-house 'look' was once again fashionable, whether in a country or town house. This was largely due to the lead given by Laura Ashley, who had introduced a whole generation to an updated version of the style.

One possible way to show off traditional style in its 1980s reincarnation is to arrange rooms as though the house has been in the same family for generations: this gives an opportunity to include a mixture of furniture, with some that might always have been present and newer pieces introduced from time to time over the years, in a variety of period styles.

AN UPDATED ELIZABETHAN ROOM

I chose to set this 1980s-style room in an Elizabethan room box made from a kit plus a panelling kit, and found it a very enjoyable exercise. To convert it into a country-house library, one wall is covered with bookcases. This is a *trompe l'oeil* effect (the art of painting views and objects to make them appear three-dimensional) using a picture, but wooden shelves with real miniature books would fit equally well against the panelling.

▲The portrait of Queen Elizabeth I which hung over the fireplace before the room was updated.

◀ An Elizabethan room furnished with a mixture of Tudor and modern pieces looks stunning.

▲ This room has all the key elements of 1980s style. There is a lovely blend of pastel colours and just the right mixture of over-scale ornaments.

▶ The exotic elephant ornament, by a British maker, simulates an expensive souvenir that might have been brought back from a trip to India.

The planked oak floor would have been there originally, but a Turkish carpet creates additional comfort. Large sofas – one a Victorian reproduction of a Knole sofa and one modern – and a low table to hold drinks and cigars make this a gentleman's retreat.

The tapestry remains, but the portrait of Queen Elizabeth I has been banished to a corridor. In its place is a portrait of the present owner's wife, painted by Matisse soon after their marriage, a commission that I imagine he occasionally regrets.

THE NEWLY DECORATED ROOM

A room decorated and furnished in the 1980s to simulate the country-house ideal was somewhat different but equally comfortable and attractive. Expensive patterned wallpapers were complemented by lavishly draped curtains with tasselled tie-backs, a little

over-length and allowed to trail on the floor. Pale carpets and traditional furniture styles featured strongly.

For those who had them, inherited antiques, landscape paintings and portraits of ancestors decorated the walls. Huge squashy sofas were considered essential and a grand fireplace looked both welcoming and impressive. The essence of this look was casual comfort.

The country-house style works best in a reasonably large room; mine measures 11in (280mm) H x 15in (380mm) L x 9½in (240mm) D. The room has a full-length French window fitted to the back wall, giving a view on to a pretty courtyard beyond: both French window and courtyard are part of a *trompe l'oeil* effect.

Reproduce pale-coloured fitted carpet with woollen dress fabric; a sample of a full-size wallpaper with a scroll pattern will be more suitable than a miniaturized version. Fit Georgian-style skirting board and cornice, painted white.

◄► English eighteenth-century japanned furniture, made to mimic Chinese lacquer, suits the country house and can be used in a sitting room, hall or bedroom. These eye-catching miniatures are copied from original designs.

CREATE A VIEW

A good view through a fake window can be arranged to enhance any dolls' house room – a variety of suggestions appear throughout this book. Choose a townscape or countryside view from a magazine picture to suit your room.

1 Glue your chosen picture on to card, using an all-purpose glue (not paper glue, which causes crinkles). Then fix the pictured scene, on its card backing, to the wall. Cover with acetate sheet to simulate window glazing.

2 French windows do not need a complete window frame, as the sides can be hidden by curtains and held in place by a wooden or fabric pelmet at the top.

3 Make a small step at the base of the window to give a neat finish at floor level.

4 Use a sample of upholstery fabric to make curtains to give the appearance of heavy drapes. A slightly over-scale pattern will add to the lavish effect. Turn in the side edges and a hem at the lower edge, and glue in place rather than stitching, which on thick fabric might make a ridge.

MAKE A FIREPLACE

A ready-made fireplace in cast resin could be used; for example one with an Adam-style 'marble' surround. Another good choice could be a plainer Georgian style. I decided to be economical and provide my own, using pieces of wood moulding left over from other projects.

This fireplace was designed for show rather than to appear functional; it is fitted directly onto the wall without a chimneybreast or aperture for a grate. This is a convenient and effective arrangement if you want to add a fireplace to an existing room without having to change the wallpaper.

For greater realism, fit a chimneybreast to allow depth for a grate before papering the walls, following the method given in the Edwardian section (see page 41).

▼ The blue and white china is French; these pieces came from the souvenir shop at Monet's Garden at Giverny. As arranged on the mantelshelf and hearth, they emphasize the summery look of the room.

TO MAKE THE FIREPLACE

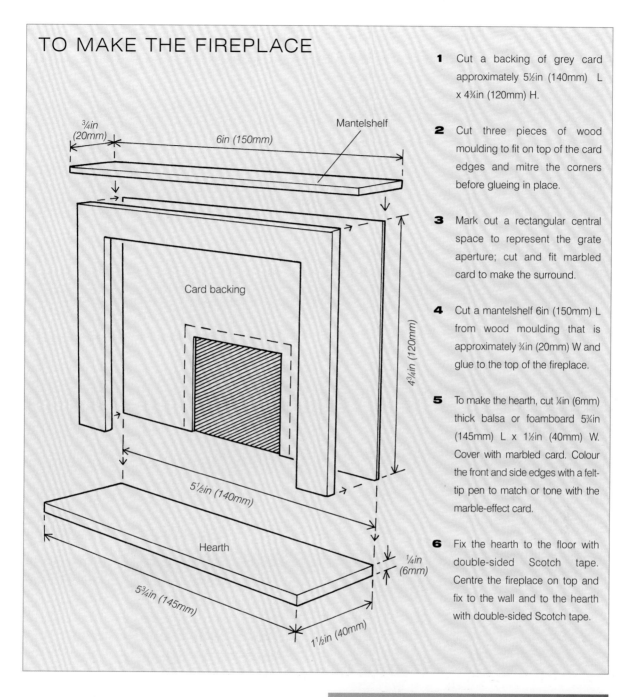

1 Cut a backing of grey card approximately 5½in (140mm) L x 4¾in (120mm) H.

2 Cut three pieces of wood moulding to fit on top of the card edges and mitre the corners before glueing in place.

3 Mark out a rectangular central space to represent the grate aperture; cut and fit marbled card to make the surround.

4 Cut a mantelshelf 6in (150mm) L from wood moulding that is approximately ¾in (20mm) W and glue to the top of the fireplace.

5 To make the hearth, cut ¼in (6mm) thick balsa or foamboard 5¾in (145mm) L x 1½in (40mm) W. Cover with marbled card. Colour the front and side edges with a felt-tip pen to match or tone with the marble-effect card.

6 Fix the hearth to the floor with double-sided Scotch tape. Centre the fireplace on top and fix to the wall and to the hearth with double-sided Scotch tape.

LIGHTING

A chandelier, whether working or non-lighting, is almost obligatory for the 1980s room. It became fashionable to twine the chain with ribbon in imitation of eighteenth-century practice. The non-working chandelier in my room is a ready-made trimming of glass beads attached to ribbon, bought from a haberdashery department.

▶ Some examples of non-working table lamps with bead bases and shades made from ribbon.

Large table lamps with drum shades were also used in the 1980s, and it is quite easy to make a non-working version of such a lamp at minimal expense.

MAKE A TABLE LAMP

1 Choose a suitably shaped bead for the base and 1in (25mm) wide velvet or thick silk ribbon to make the shade.

2 For the shade, cut a piece of cork ¾in (20mm) H – this will be covered with ribbon to create the cylindrical shape of the drum shade.

3 Cut a piece of 1in (25mm) W ribbon, long enough to go around the cork. Glue it on, taking care not to mark the ribbon – it is best to spread the glue on to the cork, leave it to become slightly tacky, then fit the ribbon. Butt the ribbon ends together and keep the join at the back when placing the lamp in a room.

4 Cut a piece of thin metal rod the length of the bead and shade, plus a little extra. Check the height of the bead base and smear a small amount of glue on to the metal rod to slightly less than this measurement. Now push the rod through the central hole of the bead and tape over the lower end to hold the rod in place while the glue sets. Finally, push the top of the metal rod into the centre of the cork, using a thimble for safety.

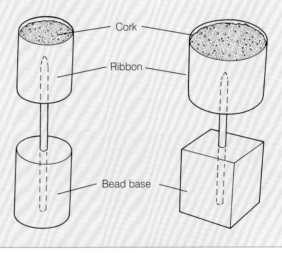

Cork

Ribbon

Bead base

◀ A country-style kitchen was desirable, whether the home was actually in the country or in town. This furniture is hand-painted with farmyard animals and birds.

THE COUNTRY KITCHEN

The Laura Ashley influence extended to the kitchen, which came to be recognized as the focus of home life, used for family meals and dinner parties as well as for cooking. More people really did cook in the 1980s; convenience food in the form of ready-meals had not yet become accepted and people enjoyed preparing elaborate dishes.

For realism, use ceramic tiles for the kitchen floor; floor-paper printed with a tile design is an acceptable alternative. Plain walls decorated with a floral or leafy border will continue the 1980s countryside theme, and the border can also surround a window so that curtains will be unnecessary.

▶ The latest four-oven Aga with lids that can be opened would add distinction to any kitchen large enough to accommodate it. It is available in similar colours to those used on the real cookers, and can be supplied fully finished or as a kit.

▲ A well-filled dresser is the centrepiece of the country kitchen. Crockery by several makers is displayed on the shelves.

◀ The open window provides a view on to a pretty courtyard. The matching set of washing-up bowl, bin and plate rack adds an authentic touch, as dishwashers were not always present in the British kitchen in the 1980s. The shelves below the sink provide convenient storage for baskets or pots.

In the American kitchen you would find the latest modern cooker, but a British country-style kitchen was incomplete without an Aga (a modern range) if it could be afforded. It was a status symbol, but it did also keep the kitchen warm. The Aga in the kitchen shown is a double-oven version from an inexpensive range of dolls' house furniture.

It was in the 1980s that the Belfast sink made its comeback. Twenty years earlier, people had been anxious to dispose of them as Victorian relics and install a new stainless steel model.

▲ A kitchen table looks its best if it is laid out with some fresh food in preparation.

▼ This fine example of 1/12 hexagonal patchwork was professionally made. If you're skilled with a needle, you can sew your own from a kit which includes tiny templates.

BEDROOMS AND BATHROOMS

A bedroom lavishly draped with floral-patterned fabric is appropriate, and a quilt on the bed will be the centrepiece. There was a revival of interest in patchwork at this time, and it became a popular hobby for those keen on sewing.

◀ The country-house ambience can be extended into the bathroom. A ready-made fitment with a deep washbasin set into a marble-topped cupboard will provide a suitable feeling of opulence.

THE 1990s

During the 1990s the trend to renovate older properties continued, and some new homes were built in the style of former periods. Like the conversions, they were fitted out with the latest in modern technology. As one example, homes that follow original Shaker style were built along the eastern seaboard of America. Few people are lucky enough to own one, but you can achieve your wildest dreams in miniature.

UPDATING THE PERIOD HOUSE

If you already have a period-style dolls' house and plan some alterations to the interior, it is worth bearing in mind that you can change the decorations and include contemporary furniture in a miniature home of any date from Tudor to nineteenth century, while leaving the façade untouched. This can revitalize a tired-looking scheme or transform a house that needs interior decoration and renovation.

▲ The spacious, light-filled rooms are as seductive as an empty loft space to even the most committed modernist. The dolls' house would look equally good furnished with Shaker-style miniatures or the latest twenty-first-century designs.

▼ This 1/12 Shaker house with external clapboarding and working sash windows is available ready-built or as a set of plans and a parts kit for the keen woodworker.

The MODERN Dolls' House

Here is an ancient-looking dolls' house that has been converted for modern living. It is modelled on a sixteenth-century yeoman's dwelling, that has even earlier origins.

► This appealing, timber-framed dolls' house is in 1/24 scale but can also be made in 1/12. The brickwork and plaster finish, hand-painted in realistic colours, is delightful.

▲ The interior of the 'Yeoman's house' is now arranged as a family home in a country style that has a mixture of old and new furniture.

► There is just enough space to park a single pushchair in the hallway of the 1/24 house. Here is a double buggy for the larger home; it is a miniaturized version of a 1990s design, with a rack to hold the shopping.

MODERN ADDITIONS

The house has been arranged to suit a modern family, with a country-style kitchen complete with an Aga, a cottage-style living room and a bedroom, which includes some antique furniture. The nursery has plenty of children's toys and the pushchair in the hall adds to the lived-in effect. The old Victorian range in the inglenook has been kept as an attractive feature.

OPEN A GALLERY

Another use for an updated period dolls' house is as a combined work and living space. One good way to display a small collection of similar miniatures, or furniture and accessories left over after a change of

▼ This comfortable living room is part of a conversion of a medieval mill house as a weekend home which would provide rest and relaxation for city dwellers.

◄ Later, I transformed the room to make a gallery to display handmade pottery. This is mostly in 1/24, although the floor-standing pieces are in 1/12. The room has a quiet, timeless quality and is just right to show the work of a country potter.

style, is to begin on a gallery. Living accommodation can be arranged in a room above or below the gallery display space, provided there is a well-placed staircase for access.

Such a gallery might specialize in antiques, art, ceramics, 1930s furniture, crafts … choose your own theme. During the 1990s a record number of art and craft galleries opened and most seem to be still thriving, so this is a topical project.

Compare the two versions of the interior of the little mill house on page 103 – I find it hard to choose which I enjoy most – which do you like best?

▼ In a family home, a childproof bathroom is essential. This simple arrangement would suit a country house, with its plain tiled floor (squared paper) and tongue-and-groove panelling. The splashback behind the basin is a piece of textured card.

A HOME FOR THE 1990s

Most new homes were built with state-of-the-art kitchens and bathrooms. Each family used the available space differently to suit their needs, but a home office and a television room became more common than a separate dining room or a designated guest room, and children's playrooms replaced traditional nurseries.

You may like to model the interior of a modern dolls' house on your own home as it looked through the 1990s. What you include will be limited by the number of rooms. Decide on your priorities before you begin.

KITCHENS AND BATHROOMS
A kitchen and a bathroom are essential for the modern dolls' house. Pictured below and on the facing page are some examples.

▲ Deep blue storage units and the latest range-style cooker complete with aluminium hood suit the upmarket modern kitchen.

◄ The dark blue porcelain bowl looks striking against the black and white background. The floor covering is squared paper.

HOME OFFICE

The modern trend of working from home and for computers to become part of our everyday lives means that the home office is now common. It can be in a hallway or on a landing, in a corner of a larger room or extended to fill the whole of a small room if you can spare one.

Home computers, photocopiers, filing cabinets and filing systems are all available in 1/12 scale so that miniaturists can reproduce their home office in their dolls' house.

▲ All the essentials for the home office can be fitted into a small space.

A CHILDREN'S PLAYROOM

A modern children's playroom can be fun to decorate. Choose bright colours for the walls and floor, and add stickers and cartoon-character images from television shows, films and books. These are available from most stationers and toy shops.

▼ Transform a plain cupboard into a magical one in minutes by adding stickers showing wizards and conjuring tricks. The wizard on the cupboard front is an appliqué motif from a haberdashers. For economy, this cupboard is of white card.

▲ There is plenty to keep children occupied in this playroom. Animal stickers on the walls are placed at a low level for a child's eye view, and the bunk beds allow two children to share the space.

▶ Inexpensive bunk beds are supplied complete with bedding. In the dolls' house they can be used to display toys or to accommodate child dolls.

SHOPS

And now we come to the great pastime of the 1990s – shopping. This era saw the transformation of shops, especially department stores and malls, so that what had been simple retail outlets additionally became places of entertainment. Families took to shopping together for a day out, not only to make essential purchases but to admire the displays and in-store demonstrations and to stop for refreshments before returning home.

▼ A department store made by a Scottish miniaturist group; each member provided a specialist department.

A shop is a useful display space for the miniaturist too, and shops are often chosen as a project for a dolls' house club, so that the members can enjoy themselves making their own speciality, whether it is tiny hats, woodturnings or food made from Fimo.

A shop can be arranged in a very small space, and one idea that has become popular recently is to make a shop in a stationery box-file. The main part of the box can be used for shelving and some of the stock, while a larger floor area can be provided by the box lid. It is necessary to remove the spring clip to allow the floor to lie flat.

▲ The fascia board and the bright paint colour on the façade of this fancy dress shop will attract attention. A single-storey shop allows ample space for the stock; but choose one with living accommodation above if you want to tackle a larger project.

▶ A pet shop is an idea that will appeal to an animal lover. A non-opening door at the back suggests a storeroom beyond.

RESURRECT AN OLD IDEA

Toy sweet shops, generally made of cardboard, used to be popular with children and were given as Christmas presents in the 1930s, stocked with a variety of real sweets in tiny glass jars that could be refilled. I have not seen one of these for many years, but a sweet shop is an unusual idea for a miniature project.

◀ A sweet shop can be filled with beautifully packaged confectionery and chocolates. Here are some appetizing-looking examples, made by a professional miniaturist.

◀ Another unusual idea is a Christmas shop, now a year-round fixture in many towns and cities.

Ideas for the
New Century

Part 3

THE TWENTY-FIRST CENTURY

At the beginning of the twenty-first century, houses designed to look to the future rather than the past are at last widely accepted – both full-scale and in miniature. Miniaturists who had previously concentrated on earlier styles now also make ultra-modern dolls' houses and furniture as well as period designs, and this has been welcomed by hobbyists eager to try something new. The start of a new millennium seemed to make us all more adventurous.

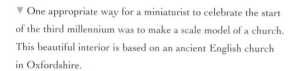

▼ One appropriate way for a miniaturist to celebrate the start of the third millennium was to make a scale model of a church. This beautiful interior is based on an ancient English church in Oxfordshire.

▲ Commissioned by a London dolls' house shop to encourage hobbyists to look to the future, the most striking feature of this 'high-tech' house is the central, full-height glazed area which allows a tantalizing glimpse of some of the contents.

▼ The light, spacious hallway is both welcoming and attractive, and the semi-open plan gives views of other areas. The open stairs are fitted with a metal safety rail and good use is made of the understairs space.

▲ This twenty-first-century house has six rooms and incorporates the most up-to-date lighting and designer touches that any modernist could desire. It can be made to order, to furnish to your own choice.

▼The kitchen is finished with stylish aluminium wall panels, ceiling-mounted spotlights and an up-to-date cooker and hood. Naturally, there is also a dishwasher and a capacious wine rack waiting to be filled.

◄ The bedroom has a calm atmosphere, adaptable lighting and a hint of Japanese style in the wall covering, which resembles a shoji screen.

DECORATING THE MODERN DOLLS' HOUSE

The modern dolls' house has many features that simplify decoration.

- A flat roof is easier to deal with than a sloping roof. The complication of slates or tiles is largely avoided; a parapet of plain stripwood makes a neat finish, and the flat roof space can be turned into a garden or even be used to add a swimming pool.

- External door casings and window frames can be made of plain stripwood rather than elaborate mouldings, so it is not essential to mitre corners.

- A painted finish to represent plaster or concrete instead of brick or stone cladding makes completion of the façade straightforward.

- Internal doorways may have simple cut-out spaces, so there is no need to provide a door frame.

- Skirting boards are an anachronism: instead, the walls of a full-scale twenty-first-century house may be indented at the base to avoid scuff marks. In 1/12 or 1/24, this detail is unnecessary, as it will be too small to need emphasis.

- Fireplaces are optional: if you prefer, you can install a central heating radiator based on one of the latest models. (I recently saw one that looked just like a giant paper clip: other suggestions for providing fake radiators are given on page 116.)

MAKE A TOWN HOUSE

Affordable houses in towns are designed to suit limited spaces. Many three-storey homes are built as infill, just like the Victorian terraced houses that may flank them, but designed in a minimalist style that is easy to maintain.

As a contrast to the spacious modern dolls' house shown at the start of this section, here is a project to make a small town house in 1/24 scale that is easy to assemble, decorate and furnish. No tools are needed.

By definition, a dolls' house with two or more rooms is made up of a series of boxes. There are many

▲ A rooftop swimming pool set in the calm atmosphere of a Zen garden is both attractive and unusual.

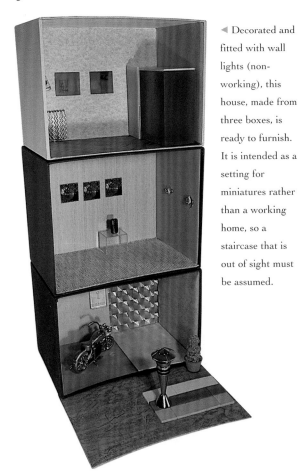

◀ Decorated and fitted with wall lights (non-working), this house, made from three boxes, is ready to furnish. It is intended as a setting for miniatures rather than a working home, so a staircase that is out of sight must be assumed.

possible variations, but the most straightforward is the two- or three-storey house with a single room on each floor. The house can be open-fronted so that the interior will be on show to make a decorative addition to your home.

The house demonstrates what can be achieved by using three similar-sized boxes. Each measures 9¼in (235mm) wide by 6in (150mm) deep; two are 6¼in (160mm) high and the third 7in (180mm) high, allowing a useful variation in room height. These boxes once held sets of books, but you can use any strong, rigid boxes of a suitable size. They all need to be the same width and depth to make a neat house when stacked.

Boxes all of the same colour will give a uniform appearance to the house exterior; the alternative is to colour-coordinate each room to the outside of its box, which will emphasize the modern style.

I imagined a small executive-type house designed to suit a young professional couple, who in real life would probably move on to something larger when they start a family. The conventional upmarket decorations mean that it would be easily resaleable, so again this house is true to modern life. I see it as a show home, so have included only token furnishings to convey a lifestyle image.

The lower storey is treated as a parking space plus utility room and entrance. The middle floor is the main sitting room, and the top floor is the bedroom with en suite shower.

INTERIOR DECORATIONS

All the rooms are finished using art papers, wallpaper samples and textured card, rather than more conventional materials or paint. The ceilings are papered with plain white paper to reflect light. I chose a variety of subtle shades and textures, bearing in mind that the house is open-fronted – sudden colour clashes might spoil the overall effect. Colour accents are provided by small pictures on the walls.

▶ In the sitting room, thick textured paper makes a floor that simulates sisal carpet. The wall lights are children's hair ornaments.

There is no need to buy a large sheet of art paper every time. Most suppliers sell offcuts, and also offcuts of art mounting board and card at a fraction of the regular price. Sizes are often just what is needed for a miniature project.

◀ The lower floor provides a parking space for a superior motor bike (a novelty clock – the dial is concealed on the reverse side). The fake entrance door is made from holographic card that illuminates the parking area with reflected light from outside the house.

In such small rooms, neat, modern central heating radiators are preferable to fireplaces as they take up little space: this is standard practice in many new town houses. In the sitting room, the radiator attached to the wall is a picture of a new design, taken from an advertisement. The bedroom radiator is made from a set of coloured hairgrips, fixed on to a pastel-coloured card backing.

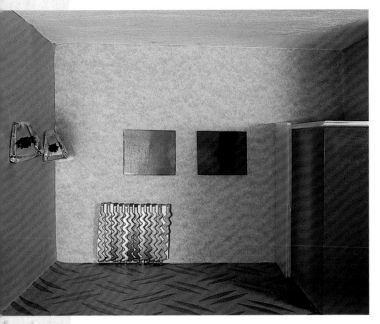

▲The shower is a semi-translucent, coloured resin candleholder, with a door added at one side to extend the fitment to make an en suite shower room. The door is made of white reeded card, which is also used to make a top for the fitment.

Near to the gleaming fake entrance door on the lower floor, there is a glass key plate engraved with the words 'New Home' (see page 115). You will be able to find something similar in a craft gallery or gift shop. It prompted the thought that this house project might make an unusual present for friends or family who are moving house in real life.

INTERIOR DESIGN IN THE TWENTY-FIRST CENTURY

By 2001, interior decoration had settled into a new style: uncarpeted hardwood floors, neutral colours and oriental influences became key features of a different look for the home. The work of leading interior designers was well publicized in home decoration magazines, read by a growing number of people, and the ideas shown in turn influenced displays in furniture stores.

Off-whites, taupe, brown and beige, spiced up with dark brown and orange or red, made a calm, restful background. Clutter was swept away, and just a few carefully chosen ornaments, preferably oriental vases, bowls or perhaps Buddha figures, could be seen to advantage in rooms with a minimal amount of furniture. The oriental influence was immediately apparent: restful and calming, so that the home could become a retreat from the ever-busier and perhaps more threatening world outside.

▲The low table and minimalist flower arrangement create a peaceful effect against the beautiful woodwork. This restful corner is part of a prize-winning room for the twenty-first century, created by a Scottish Miniaturist Group.

Natural materials had returned to favour: in the most expensive kitchens, stone floors replaced vinyl, and granite or solid wood worktops were preferred to the synthetic worktops that had lasted for years (losing some of the advantage of wipe-clean surfaces which did not stain).

▲The latest bathrooms are provided with free-standing bowls of glass, porcelain or even stone. In this design, the tap would no longer need to be turned on and off: the water would flow when a hand is placed beneath it. This is an arrangement that is sure to be here to stay. 'His' and 'Hers' bowls are, as yet, unusual in the dolls' house.

▼ Florists' buckets, each containing a single large lily, are a typical designer touch and are invariably arranged in groups of three.

▼ In the sitting room, the low, armless sofa has a wooden base topped with bronze gauzy ribbon over silver upholstery (a metallic pan cleaner) which shines through the gauze. The soft, shaggy cushions are made from children's hairbands.

These decorative ideas all look wonderful in miniature rooms, without the sometimes prohibitive expense of the originals. Neutral does not mean dull: the blend of pale colours can be given variety by the use of textured fabrics. The most expensive sofas are covered in suede and strewn with velvet or shaggy cushions, sometimes adorned with tassels; fabrics that glisten with gold thread are another subtle way to complement a predominantly beige room. These ideas are all easy to scale down.

A ZEN-STYLE APARTMENT

Colloquially, the new decorative ideas became known as Zen style. It reached inner cities first, where old industrial buildings continued to be converted into expensive and well-designed apartments. The modern minimalist apartment gives another opportunity for the hobbyist to make and decorate scenes in room boxes as an alternative to a complete dolls' house.

The room settings in my 'apartment' convey the essence of oriental-influenced Western style. Each room is 10½in (270mm) high by 10in (255mm) deep; the sitting room is 12½in (315mm) wide and the bedroom slightly smaller at 11in (280mm) wide.

THE SITTING ROOM

The pale woodstrip flooring is paper, and the textured cream wallpaper on the back wall is a sample of regular-size wallpaper that has a slightly raised pattern resembling foliage. To achieve a similar look, add variety with a mix of textures and keep furniture to a minimum, so that what is there can make an impact.

ADD A BOWL FIRE

The ultra-modern feature is the flame-effect fire with tiny pebbles, rather than the more usual simulated coal, arranged in a shallow bowl. Arrange your own 'flames' with red or orange paper: I used a cut-out from a picture advertising this type of 'living flame' fire, but red and orange cellophane is an effective alternative. The fire stands directly on the hearth where it shows up well, rather than being set back.

▶ The completed fireplace with the latest style of fire bowl. The miniature pots on either side are based on modern Japanese porcelain. The fireplace wall is papered in cream with a faint stripe to emphasize this arrangement.

MAKE A FIREPLACE

As is so often the case, the focal point of the sitting room is the fireplace. Make one to suit the room from thick black card (or wood, painted matt black). The hearth is of black and gold marble-effect card, while the fireback is pale grey to provide contrast and lighten the effect.

1 Cut balsa wood or foamboard approximately ½in (13mm) thick, 3¼in (85mm) H x 3¾in (95mm) W. Cut out a central rectangle 1¾in (45mm) H x 2⅛in (55mm) W for the grate aperture.

2 Colour all the edges with a black felt-tip pen, including the edges of the aperture.

3 Cover the fireplace with black card. (Note: when cutting the pieces for front, sides and top, they should be fractionally larger than the base so that the card joins do not show.)

4 Cut a piece of pale grey card ½in (13mm) larger all round than the size of the grate aperture and glue to the back of the fireplace to make a fireback.

5 Cut a hearth from ¼in (6mm) thick card or wood, 1½in (40mm) W x 4in (100mm) L, and cover with marbled card. Colour the edges with a gold pen. Fit to the floor with double-sided Scotch tape. Fit the fireplace centrally over the hearth.

THE BEDROOM

Like the sitting room, the bedroom has a contrasting paper on the end wall, in this case a pale orange art paper with a textured finish. The doorway towards the back of the room is fitted with an acetate screen that allows plenty of light to filter through from the sitting room.

In modern loft apartments, doorways are sometimes left completely open and no door is provided, but in a dolls'-house-size apartment the transparent infill can make it look properly finished, although this is an optional feature.

THE FURNITURE AND ACCESSORIES

A bed and a table are all that is needed to furnish the bedroom. A wooden soap tray makes a base for the bed. Add a bamboo headboard – mine was part of the handle from a soft brush (made in China) – or you can cut one from a thick bamboo tablemat. I used a bought lavender bag, made of brown velvet, as a duvet: this has the advantage of scenting the room.

▲The flame-effect fire bowl filled with a layer of pebbles is simple to arrange.

▼The low table is the top of an ornamental soapstone box, used to display the delicate orchid in a translucent porcelain vase. The leaves attached to the wall are from an Indian peepul tree; they can occasionally be found in shops that stock art papers, or in gift shops.

ETHNIC INFLUENCES

An interest in miniature scale can extend to a variety of subjects. In the main, hobbyists tend to concentrate on projects that they can study in their own locality, but it can be rewarding to try schemes based on more exotic styles. This gives an opportunity to plan a decorative scheme that may be very different from those nearer to home, and to gain a small insight into other cultures.

A CHINESE TEMPLE

A temple interior is a place for calm concentration, richly decorated with symbols of Buddhism and containing gilded artefacts. One room from such a temple makes an interesting project that can begin with a choice of background paper (giftwrap) showing Chinese characters and symbols, and allow for the inclusion of a few small objects obtained from gift or museum shops.

▼ The temple interior is serene and beautiful. The gilded Buddha figure was sculpted by a professional miniaturist, and the Chinese-style carpet is one from a dolls' house range. The soapstone lions guarding the entrance came from an oriental gift shop.

▲ A miniature lacquer screen from China, with panels that depict the four seasons. The screen is in 1/10 scale, but not too large to use in a dolls' house.

JAPANESE STYLE

Japan is a contradiction; alongside the traditional home with its sparsely furnished, low-ceilinged rooms and small courtyard there are modern apartments that are equipped with the latest technology.

The Japanese love miniature replicas of dolls, furniture, houses and gardens, and just as in the West, the dolls' house hobby is popular. It differs in that because homes in general are small, 1/24 is

the preferred scale and, using traditional origami techniques, even young children are adept at making tiny replicas of dolls and furniture in exquisite detail.

A TRADITIONAL JAPANESE ROOM

To get the best effect with minimal decoration, choose textures and colours of papers carefully. Real Japanese papers can be found in shops specializing in art papers.

The bathroom is a very important part of any Japanese home. If you decide to extend your Japanese room box by adding on further rooms, this should take priority. A deep tub is essential and typically would be rectangular and made of wood. But even though many Japanese keep to a traditional style in part of their home, a more modern bathroom may now be chosen.

A MODERN TOKYO APARTMENT

In contrast to the traditional room, you might enjoy arranging a modern interior. An apartment in Tokyo is often a very small space indeed and will probably belong to a young professional. The home looks inwards, away from the bustle of the city, and from the outside the apartment block will show only a plain concrete façade with few windows facing the street.

Decorations should feature grey, black or brown, with red, orange or yellow colour accents. The floors may be of wood or of matting. All Japanese woodwork is beautifully finished, so if you choose wood, a piece of veneer from a craft shop would be preferable to a paper simulation. Alternatively, use part of a woven straw tablemat to provide a textured

▶ Made in Japan: two handmade lidded jars bought at an English miniatures fair.

▲ Irises in a shallow bowl are displayed on a red silk-covered box in this traditional-style gold and black room. The print on the wall was cut from a magazine.

▲ An idea for an updated Japanese bathroom: this bathtub is a deep soapstone box. The porcelain basin sits on a wooden shelf and there is a view of the garden.

appearance similar to tatami matting (thick, rectangular, woven straw mats, used as floor covering in traditional Japanese rooms).

For the walls of my room I decided on a glossy bronze paper with a hint of mauve to suit the idea of a sophisticated city apartment. Pale grey would also make a good background.

Of necessity, such a tiny living space has to be kept tidy: this is often difficult in reality, and the modern Japanese apartment can be cluttered. However, this is not a problem in miniature, where boxes or low cupboards can be assumed to hold anything that does not have to be kept out for immediate use.

Use a small box to make a cupboard. I used a black card box with a grey pull-out inside. Punch a hole in the centre of the pull-out drawer, as handles are not attached in Japan. A low shelf can be arranged as a display space. To make the shelf, use a piece of wood or a long, shallow box, painted grey.

Japanese rooms frequently consist of a curious mixture of treasured objects and quirky, individual modern items. Given the general admiration for pop music and footballers, there may be anything from a poster with a picture of David Beckham to a collection of mechanical toys. Whatever you choose to put in your room, remember that the obligatory television set is always placed on the floor or a low shelf, where it will be at eyelevel for someone sitting on a cushion or mat.

▶ Miniature lacquerwork is still made in Japan, copied from full-size traditional pieces. Look for those that include mother of pearl, which is often a feature of top-quality lacquerwork. This set of stacking boxes on a tray is a typical design.

▼ This room measures 7in x 7in x 7in (180mm x 180mm x 180mm), an exact cube. It includes both a modern painting and a Japanese print depicting a Kabuchi Theatre actor. The tiny figure of a Samurai warrior is a startling contrast to the miniature robot clock. On the low shelf, a teapot and two teabowls are ready for use. A porcelain stem bowl contains the flower without which no Japanese interior is complete.

ADD A COURTYARD

However tight the space, even a single-room apartment might have at least a token courtyard to provide the essential link with nature. It could be just a narrow, gravelled strip against one wall, with three strategically placed rocks or a single pot plant. If there is simply no space in the main room, this may be fitted in the entrance hall or along a corridor.

To make a room with an attached courtyard you will need to omit one solid side wall from the main room. This will be replaced by a wall of reeded envelope stiffener or acetate sheet to divide the room from the courtyard. The room size is again 7in x 7in x 7in (180mm x 180mm x 180mm).

▲ Extra rooms can be added to this project easily. The bathroom might be next in importance: here is an idea to suit a modern city apartment.

▲ A bamboo blind allows light to filter into the room from the courtyard.

1 Cut a baseboard 9½in (240mm) L x 7in (180mm) D. This will allow a space 2½in (65mm) W x 7in (180mm) D for the courtyard.

2 To make the courtyard walls and ceiling, first cut the glazing: one piece 2½in (65mm) W x 7in (180mm) H for the back wall, two pieces 7in (180mm) L x 7in (180mm) H for the side walls, one piece 7¼in (185mm) L x 2¾in (70mm) W for the ceiling. (Note: the ceiling is larger as it will cover the back and side walls.)

3 Glue the glazing to the side of the room, as shown in the diagram.

4 Next, make the gravelled floor to the courtyard.

a) Cut a piece of card 2⅜in (60mm) W x 6⅞in (175mm) L.

b) Spread evenly with white PVA wood glue and cover with florists' decorative sand in a grey-green colour, pressing down firmly and evenly to make a flat surface.

c) When the glue is dry, turn the floor upside down and shake it gently to remove any surplus. Repeat the process if necessary to fill in any bald patches.

d) Slide the gravelled floor into the courtyard space.

5 Glue the completed room plus courtyard on to the base board.

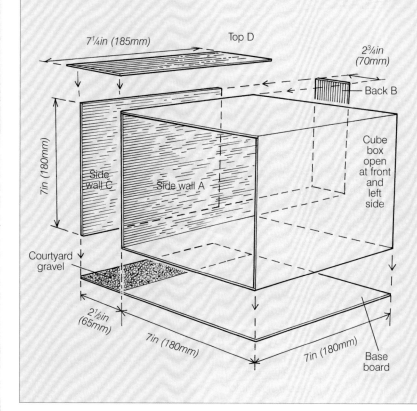

7¼in (185mm)

Top D

2¾in (70mm)

Back B

7in (180mm)

Cube box open at front and left side

Side wall C

Side wall A

Courtyard gravel

2½in (65mm)

7in (180mm)

7in (180mm)

Base board

A PLAYROOM FOR A JAPANESE CHILD

With home space so cramped in many parts of Japan, it would be a lucky child who had a designated playroom. Japanese toys are so appealing that it seemed a pity not to make such a room which I felt a Japanese child would enjoy – but the room is necessarily minimal compared with a Western playroom.

Japanese children are fascinated by cartoon characters and video games from an early age. Therefore, in a room designed to suit a slightly older child it would be appropriate to include a television set or computer.

▼Bright colours enliven the room for a Japanese child. The tiny Emperor and Empress dolls are traditionally displayed for the annual Girls' Festival.

▼The dolls displayed on the low units were all made in Japan while the toy-box was bought in England from a gift shop. To bring nature into the room, a flat porcelain dish contains two colourful leaves.

AN INDIAN EXTRAVAGANZA

India is another country that always seems exotic to Westerners. The heat, the colours, the noise and, more recently, the influence of 'Bollywood', a film industry that now attracts worldwide attention, are all a great contrast to Western-style living.

MAKE A BOLLYWOOD-STYLE ROOM

Replicating a Bollywood-style room allows the freedom to include far more blatant luxury than in most miniature scenes. This room setting is based on the apartment belonging to a famous Indian film star; in 2002 a replica of part of the apartment went on show at an exhibition in a London department store, where it attracted a record number of visitors. Lavishly decorated in vivid colours, filled with silver furniture and accessorized with silk cushions, mirrors and jewels, it was greeted with general astonishment. Part of the enjoyment in recreating this room is in the ingenious use of non-dolls'-house bits and pieces to complete the effect.

The centrepiece of the room is an elaborate bed with its jewelled headboard. To recreate this, use a gift box as the bed base, preferably in deep pink or purple, or cover a plain box with shiny paper. The bedcover is a metallic pan cleaner, while jewelled finials are plastic hair ornaments. A jewelled Indian mirror frame is used as a headboard. Unless you want to take a picture of your

▼ The silver furniture used in this 'Bollywood' room is inexpensive white wire furniture (made in China and widely available from both dolls' house shops and department stores), transformed with silver model enamel. The leopard is a toy shop animal, painted silver to look like a statue, while the jewelled boxes were from a gift shop.

▼ Art papers and giftwrap are used for floors and walls. Purple, orange and hot pink combine well, and tassels and braid add finishing touches.

room, the mirror could be left in place, but as it can cause unwanted reflections in photographs, I removed it and instead covered a piece of card with multi-coloured braid to put in the frame.

THE INDIAN COURTYARD

In India, an apartment of this degree of luxury would have its own private courtyard, probably floored in marble and with a canopied area to provide shade. For the flooring I used a textured paper with a raised pattern of flowers and leaves which look as though they are scattered on the surface.

An alternative could be mosaic tiles, which can be simulated with paint, paper or card. The rough-textured background paper combines colours in a manner that is almost three-dimensional to achieve a scenic effect.

◄ The completed courtyard looks suitably exotic. The remarkably inexpensive elephants came from an ethnic gift shop.

▼ Transformation scene! The courtyard looks extraordinarily beautiful by moonlight, an effect achieved by a change of backdrop – a dark blue paper sprinkled with silver – and low lighting. The silver gazebo and seat are an irresistible invitation to a moonlit tryst.

SANTA FE ROOM AND COURTYARD

Santa Fe in New Mexico is a magical place both for those who live there and to holiday visitors. It combines Central American Indian culture with North American influences and has a charm all its own.

The adobe (sun-baked clay) houses in earthy colours are a major part of the attraction of Santa Fe and interesting to reproduce in miniature. Even Frank Lloyd Wright fell in love with them and designed a house with similar characteristics, although his was never built there during his lifetime.

Most houses today have been updated for modern living and have sophisticated interiors. I chose to reproduce a rustic, fairly primitive home, which conveys the feeling of an original, unmodernized dwelling.

DECORATING THE INTERIOR OF THE ROOM

Line the walls of the box with soft card or 3.5mm (approx. ⅛in) foamboard and cover with thick, coloured paper. Vary the colours: terracotta, orange, buff or ochre all work well. Wrap the paper round each piece of lining and fix it at the back with glue or sticky tape. This covering over a semi-soft base suggests the thickness of

▲The low bed is a wood and raffia soap stand and the typical Mexican musical instruments came from an ethnic gift shop. The flooring looks very realistic, although it is actually a pictured surface.

the adobe walls, as do the curved edges produced by using this method. Next fix the walls in place with double-sided Scotch tape along all the edges.

▼The one-room home is set in a large, ready-made box measuring 11in (280mm) H x 10in (255mm) D x 15¾in (400mm) W. This is a standard size of box; alternatively, make one to suit your own requirements from foamboard (see page 12).

MAKE A CORNER FIREPLACE

Corner fireplaces are a noticeable feature of Santa Fe homes. They, too, are of adobe and look chunky with rounded corners and a thick hearth.

1 First, you need to make a corner chimneybreast.

a) Cut a piece of 3.5mm (approx. ⅛in) foamboard or soft card 5in (130mm) wide and ¾in (20mm) less than the height of the room. Cut the side edges at an angle of 45° so that they will fit flush against the walls when fitted across the corner.

b) Cover with thick coloured paper to blend with the other walls.

2 Next, make the hearth and fireplace. Set the chimneybreast aside while you make the hearth; the chimneybreast will fit on top of the hearth.

a) Cut a triangular hearth to fit into the corner: 6½in (165mm) W x 5in (130mm) x 5in (130mm) each side. You will need to glue together several layers of foamboard to make a hearth about ¾in (20mm) deep. Round off the front corners.

b) Cut the fireplace 5in (130mm) W x 3in (75mm) H from foamboard; glue layers together to make a thickness of approximately ¾in (20mm). Cut out a space to take the fire.

c) Paint both hearth and fireplace with stone model enamel; apply two coats for a smooth effect on the fireplace, but aim for a rough finish on the hearth.

d) Next, cut out a space in the chimneybreast that is slightly larger than the aperture in the fireplace.

3 Glue the hearth in place, and then glue the chimneybreast on top. Finally, glue the fireplace in position against the chimneybreast and hearth and stack the logs upright, not horizontal, following local style.

Corner of room

Chimneybreast

5in (130mm)

¾in (20mm)

Fireplace

3in (75mm)

5in (130mm)

Fit chimneybreast on top of hearth

Hearth

5in (130mm)

¾in (20mm)

6½in (165mm)

▲The completed fireplace is used to show off decorated beads which can stand on end to look like pottery vases.

THE CEILING

The ceiling can be treated in the same way as the walls. In some houses ceilings are of wood, and a quick way to reproduce this alternative effect is to use a slatted table mat. It will look realistic and is easy to cut and fit in one piece. Turn the box upside down and use PVA wood glue to fix it in place. Leave until the glue is thoroughly dry before putting the box the right way up.

FIT THE FLOORING

A picture of a stone floor in earthy tones taken from a brochure may be ideal for the floor. If you prefer, simulate an earth floor by painting card with a reddish-coloured paint (brown and red make a good blend) thickened with a little interior filler to give it a grainy texture.

PERUVIAN AND MEXICAN SOUVENIRS AS ORNAMENTS

Miniature animals and figures to complete the room are widely available in ethnic gift shops. Braids and woven purses with typical designs are inexpensive and can be cut up and used for blankets and floor rugs.

Remember to include a plain wooden religious cross on the wall and some earthenware pots or jugs. A metal candlestick with a candle, and perhaps an exotic flower or a cactus in a pot, complete the room.

A SANTA FE COURTYARD

You might like to add a courtyard to your one-room house. I used the lid of a cardboard box measuring approximately 15in (380mm) long by 12in (305mm) deep, with an edging 1½in (40mm) high. Alternatively, make a base from wood or thick card and add a wall of stripwood to provide a typical fence.

▼The courtyard seems full of warmth and colour. Stepladders were used by the Pueblo Indians to reach other parts of the buildings rather than internal staircases – entry from outside was through a window aperture. They are still features of Santa Fe life today, although homes now have doors.

▶The materials used to make both room and terrace are colourful and varied. It is worth looking in gift shops and haberdashery departments to search out suitable beads and braids.

ADD STEPS

One authentic touch is to add steps to join the terrace to the house. Make steps from blocks of roughly cut balsa wood; the painted finish can be rough for this purpose.

1 Mark out the position for the steps on the terrace floor but glue them in place after the floor is complete.

2 Paint the floor and steps with an ochre-coloured matt paint. Add a tiled area near to the house: I used part of a wallpaper sample with a mosaic tile effect. Mark this area while you complete the rest of the floor.

3 To add texture to the painted surface, use ornamental sand (sold for flower arrangers and use in fish tanks) and apply as for the Japanese courtyard.

4 Finally, fit the steps in place and add some large stones and fake cacti.

MAKE A FENCE

This realistic-looking fence is typical of those around Santa Fe and can be made from emery boards or ice-lolly sticks.

1 Use ⅜in (10mm) square dowel for the corner posts, and woodstrip for the horizontal bars. Red, blue and white are the colours that are always used, arranged in sequence.

2 Paint the fence and the posts very roughly with matt model enamel, and remember to be particularly sparing with the paint at the bottom edges to

show wear. The white needs to look the most faded, with the base wood just showing through.

▲A delightfully shabby fence, which looks as though faded by strong sunlight. The distinctive colours are the traditional ones used in Santa Fe.

131

PUBLIC SPACES

I have chosen a variety of projects as examples of some of the public spaces that can be enjoyable to reproduce in miniature. Each allows the development of a theme in a very different way from that required for a purely domestic interior.

OPEN A MUSEUM

Since the start of the new millennium, there has been a tremendous increase in the number of visitors to museums: looking and learning seems set to continue as a major pastime.

In real life, the seriously wealthy often build up a vast collection, and the philanthropist may decide to endow a museum or help out with a loan exhibition. In the same way, the hobbyist with a specific interest will collect miniatures that particularly appeal to them, whether it is paintings, sculpture or a group of related objects. Such a small collection can be shown off to advantage in a specially designed setting.

▼The 1/12 modern house (see page 70) is adaptable and can be used for a wide range of purposes. In this second version, it has become a museum of vintage transport with a self-service café attached. Simple alterations to the finish and interior decorations give a very different impression from the first, domestic version.

LINKED ROOMS PROVIDE A MUSEUM AND SPACE FOR A CAFÉ

I decided on a transport museum with the emphasis on vintage motorcycles for two reasons: before it became too large for the space and transferred to the British National Exhibition Centre, the international Miniatura dolls' house fair was held at the Motorcycle Museum in

▲The motorcycle display area is sure to interest any enthusiast. The Italian scooters are miniatures of vintage models dating from the 1960s. A modern television provides an interactive display, while the pictures on the wall were taken from a newspaper.

Birmingham, England. I always took time to look at the museum exhibits as well as visit the show, and discovered that motorcycles fascinated me. 1/12 replicas of a variety of models are available in gift shops and make a good display without taking up too much space, and so the idea was born.

My museum was made from the instructions given to make the modern open-plan house (see pages 74–77) but the pillars and stepped surround to the entrance are faced with textured white card instead of plasticized brick to give it more the appearance of a public building. In place of the plain glass window walls at either end in the original version, I fitted coloured acetate sheet, and

blue and purple card rather than a pale colour for the floors. The rear walls are white to show off transport posters, cut from advertisements.

THE CAFÉ

Most museums provide refreshments for their visitors; a self-service café is a good idea, as it allows more time to look at the exhibits. Start with a long table or fitment on which to lay out the food. Plastic box lids make good trays so that the sandwiches and cakes can be arranged in sequence for the customers to help themselves, while bottles of soda water and cola look best in their own special 'cool' unit.

◄The sepia photograph of a rider in the early 1930s is an original family photograph – snapshots taken by box cameras at the time were often very tiny and can be useful in a miniature setting. This portrait adds a personal touch and is used next to the model vintage motorcycle in a special display area.

▼The table and chairs and also the crockery are all inexpensive and the food looks delicious. A water jug, glasses and cutlery are laid out on the checkout desk with a mini-computer to add up the bill.

THE MUSEUM SETTING

Do a little landscaping around your museum and café. A green space or a paved area, a path of small tiles or gravel and a few tubs of flowers make an attractive surround. This also provides a place to set up signs. Choose coloured paper that will stand out against white, and use a computer to design your own museum and café fascia boards. Select these from the wide range of fonts available on most computers: try printing in several type sizes on different-coloured background papers to decide on the best effect.

Once you are satisfied, cut out the sign and glue it to card before fixing it to the front of the building or on to a free-standing signboard.

You could choose any special interest for your museum, from miniature dolls' houses and reproductions of period toys to aeroplanes or boats, and enjoy gradually building up an individual collection. For a more intimate feeling, perhaps for a costume museum, a period-style dolls' house may provide the perfect display space.

▲The Michelin Man advertising figure next to the Museum Open sign at the entrance is sure to attract attention.

▼Here is the beginning of my next specialist museum.

A HOTEL FOYER

We all stay in hotels from time to time, on holiday or on business. You may prefer the small, intimate, private hotel or the grand, deluxe version. Either way, a hotel project is immensely enjoyable, even if you get no further than the reception area. Base it on one where you spent a fantastic holiday, or maybe one you have visited to attend a memorable function.

A luxury hotel will have a reception area that is intended to impress or amaze guests as they arrive. There need not be a lot of furniture, although, if you wish, you can provide comfortable (or stylish) armchairs and small tables.

The soft glow of working lights will create atmosphere, although in this case I dispensed with electric lighting and relied on the dazzling effect of tiny stranded metallic beads suspended across the room (an inexpensive necklace). The reeded blind is a table mat made of plasticized hollow rods.

TO MAKE THE PILLAR FOR THE CORNER SUPPORT

Pillars are often a feature of hotel reception areas; in a miniature setting they should be placed with care as they can obscure details. A solid-looking pillar (see picture at top of page 136) as a corner support works well. Measure the depth of the room and the width of the proposed blind carefully so that the pillar is a neat fit in the corner.

Cut two pieces of wood or 5mm (approx. ⅕in) thick foamboard, each 12in (305mm) high and approximately 2in (50mm) wide to suit the exact size needed and glue them together lengthwise to make an L-shape.

After the glue has set, cover with the paper of your choice and glue the pillar to the floor and ceiling.

▲Bronze and gold set the colour scheme. The flooring is giftwrap in an unusual striped pattern. The reception desk is covered with the reverse side of the same paper, a pale bronze, ensuring perfect colour coordination.

◀This palatial hotel foyer is based on one in a New York hotel in Manhattan where luxury and glamour combine. It is set in a two-sided, open-fronted room box 12in (305mm) wide x 15in (380mm) deep x 12in (305mm) high, with the third wall covered by a blind to let in light or sunshine.

THE BLIND

The type of place mat used for the blind is available in a choice of colours. It is quite heavy and needs to be anchored securely above the ceiling. Use a heavy-duty cloth tape that is very strong. After fixing the blind in place, cover the fixing tape by adding an additional layer of foamboard to form the top of the room box.

◄Light shining through the blind makes a dazzling effect in this richly decorated reception area. The pillar makes a neat finish to the corner of the room.

MAKE A RECEPTION DESK

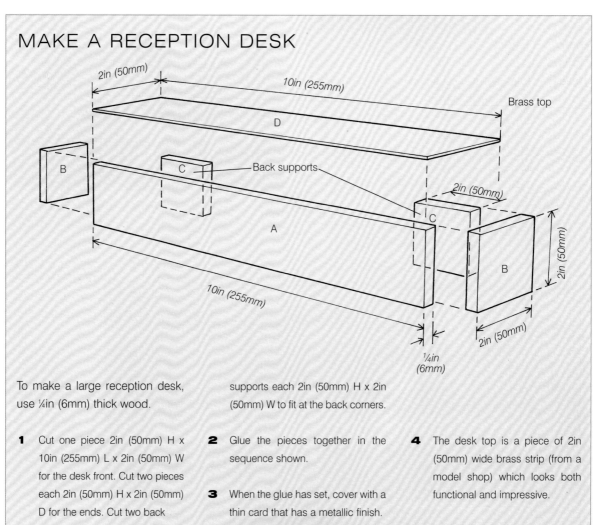

2in (50mm)
10in (255mm)
Brass top
D
B
C
Back supports
2in (50mm)
C
A
B
2in (50mm)
10in (255mm)
2in (50mm)
¼in (6mm)

To make a large reception desk, use ¼in (6mm) thick wood.

1 Cut one piece 2in (50mm) H x 10in (255mm) L x 2in (50mm) W for the desk front. Cut two pieces each 2in (50mm) H x 2in (50mm) D for the ends. Cut two back supports each 2in (50mm) H x 2in (50mm) W to fit at the back corners.

2 Glue the pieces together in the sequence shown.

3 When the glue has set, cover with a thin card that has a metallic finish.

4 The desk top is a piece of 2in (50mm) wide brass strip (from a model shop) which looks both functional and impressive.

ACCESSORIES

One or two large, striking pictures are all you need to decorate the walls. Choose 'paintings' that will complement the colour scheme. Add some imposing flower arrangements and antique ornaments to complete the extravagant and luxurious effect.

◄ Some luggage will indicate the presence of hotel guests. The trunk and suitcases are of fine-quality leather.

MAKE A LOW TABLE

As mine was to be a modern hotel, I decided on the minimalist look. The elegant modern chair is a chrome mobile phone holder, repainted as antique-effect bronze using metallic model enamel and the rub-on, rub-off method.

The low table is an open box. The inside is painted matt silver and the outside covered with bronze-coloured paper. Use a ready-made box or make one:

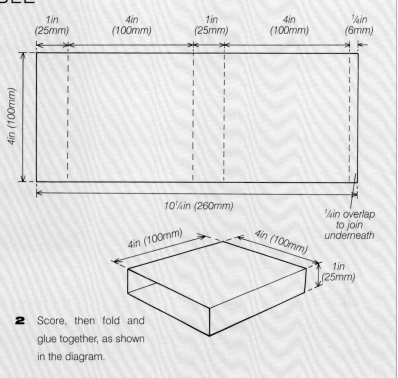

1in (25mm) 4in (100mm) 1in (25mm) 4in (100mm) ¼in (6mm)

4in (100mm)

10¼in (260mm)

¼in overlap to join underneath

4in (100mm)   4in (100mm)

1in (25mm)

1 Cut a strip of strong card that measures 10¼in (260mm) long x 4in (100mm) wide. Paint one side of the strip. This will form the inside of the table space.

2 Score, then fold and glue together, as shown in the diagram.

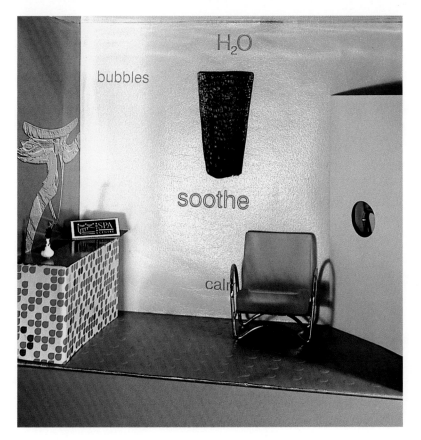

A SPA SALON RECEPTION AREA

Luxury hotels may have additional health facilities, such as swimming pools or keep-fit centres. This tiny reception is designed for a spa salon and is made in a shallow box 7in (180mm) long by 5in (130mm) deep by 8in (205mm) high. The idea for this came from the wallpaper sample with appropriate lettering on it, which gives a cool, fresh effect.

Both flooring and back wall are wallpaper samples, while the end wall is silver-grey card taken from a brochure. The door to the spa is a green plastic paper knife, which was presented in a white card pack with a small 'window' to show the green. It works well when fitted at an angle into the corner of the room.

◄ A calm, cool space is appropriate for a spa reception area.

A CHINESE RESTAURANT

A large hotel will have several top-class restaurants: a breakfast room, a tearoom, a function room, a grill room and often an oriental restaurant, so there is plenty of choice for miniaturization. To continue the theme of the grand hotel foyer, I decided on a superior Chinese restaurant, again set in a large room box.

In many new-style restaurants, the chefs can be seen preparing and cooking the food behind a glass screen, and this can be an entertainment in itself. Use a curved photograph frame as a screen: these are fitted with transparent plastic, rather than glass.

Make a 2in (50mm) high partition wall as a base for the frame; the top should be about 2in (50mm) wide to form a shelf. Arrange cooking pans behind the frame to suggest the kitchen area beyond.

THE TABLE AND ACCESSORIES

The dining table is made from two silver-grey boxes mounted on a wooden plinth painted orange-red. I have not included chairs as I wanted to show the whole scene without obscuring the table, but you might like to make banquette seating to suit the size of the table.

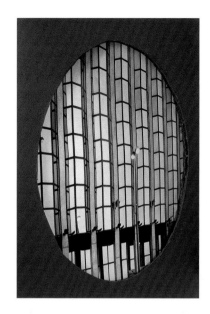

◄ This restaurant is intended as a smart city venue; the large circular window shows a view of tall buildings with plenty of glass. This is a *trompe l'oeil* effect that can work well if the picture is chosen with care.

▼ The simple but effective colour scheme is based on black, silver and an orange-red to give a suitable Chinese 'look' to the restaurant. The gleaming back wall has a repeated pattern of slightly recessed circles.

MAKE BANQUETTE SEATING

1 Cut a piece of wood 1¼in (30mm) high and the same length as the table and then paint it black.

2 Cut a piece of foam padding the same size as the top and cover it with black imitation leather, joining it underneath.

3 Glue the padded seat to the base.

NAPKINS AND CHOPSTICKS

This restaurant does not feature miniature food – there is enough drama in the spectacular interior decorations. In the kitchen behind the screen there is one token piece of salmon, but copper pans show up well and indicate that cooking will commence when the customers arrive.

To make the napkins, use thick coloured paper from a roll of kitchen towels. Cut a strip that is ¾in (20mm) wide and then cut it into ¾in (20mm) lengths. Fold each napkin diagonally to make a triangle and secure with a tiny piece of double-sided Scotch tape inside, which will not make a bump.

Used matchsticks make good chopsticks. Cut the matchstick into suitable lengths and then split each lengthwise into half and then half again. One matchstick will make two pairs of chopsticks.

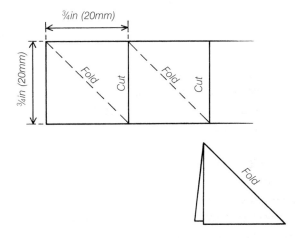

▼ A perfect table-setting, ready for the meal to begin, with a folded paper napkin and chopsticks laid neatly on each plate.

THE OFFICE

I was attracted to the idea of a minimalist working space of the kind favoured by eminent architects. It is set in an open-fronted room box with a transparent coloured plastic stationery file as part of the arrangement to provide an end wall that suggests an elevator beyond.

The room size is 12in (305mm) high, 10in (255mm) deep and 12in (305mm) long plus a 4in (100mm) long floor extension to take the stationery file at one side. The file is lined on the side facing into the room with blue holographic paper to add depth of colour and give the impression of a lit space beyond.

The office follows the American ideal of an uncluttered desk, a great view from the window, and luxurious seating for the client. Smooth, reflective surfaces predominate to give a modern appearance.

The outlook from the office is an important part of the scene. Cut a large rectangle for the window space and

▼This office is designed as though in a penthouse suite. A series of cloud pictures against a matt blue background link it with the view outside.

fit a picture behind it. The one I used is a panoramic view of London and the Thames, and emphasizes the suggestion that this office is set in the prestigious Docklands area of new development. For the partly lowered blind I used card with a striped pattern in graduations of colour. The floor is grey marbled card.

▲ One large modern armchair is ready for the client, while the desk chair is a Wassily chair, designed by Marcel Breuer and much admired by contemporary furniture designers. The plan on the wall indicates that the architect's next project may be to update the London Underground network.

MAKE THE DESK

1 You will need a wooden or strong card box approximately 5½in (140mm) long by 2½in (65mm) deep by 2¼in (60mm) high.

2 Cover the box with satin-finish grey card, curving the corners for a sleek effect.

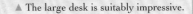

▲ The large desk is suitably impressive.

3 Make the desk top from ¼in (6mm) thick card or wood and cover it with matt grey card. I was lucky enough to find a piece with a neat blue grid pattern at one end to add interest. However, any geometric design would be suitable to glue on to plain grey card.

◄ The desk top is left bare, except for a mini-computer and a paperweight, ready to use when the architect spreads out his plans.

EXTEND THE DOLLS' HOUSE OUTDOORS

GARDEN DESIGNS FOR THE TWENTY-FIRST CENTURY

Following a trend that began in France, gardens that feature glass, metal, plastic, stone, wood and a host of natural materials but with very few real flowers, are now exhibited at major garden festivals.

When I first visited an international festival of garden design in 2002, my reaction was one of delight, astonishment, and the immediate thought that these were gardens that would adapt well to miniature scale. One advantage is that they will stay pristine and fresh-looking, just as the interior of a dolls' house stays clean and tidy.

For the owner of a modern dolls' house or an open-fronted room box, such a garden may complement your miniature home. To inspire you to share my enthusiasm, I created a few examples of low-maintenance gardens based on some innovative designs. All these gardens can be arranged in a shallow box with an edge that is approximately 1½in (40mm) or 2in (50mm) high.

A JAPANESE DRY GARDEN

The Japanese dry garden has been given a modern twist recently by innovative and influential Japanese architects and designers. My garden features pebbles, stones and gravel arranged in neat rows. A wooden platform provides an area from which to view the garden, which is intended to be admired, rather than walked on. At the far end, a low wooden wall painted black, and a bamboo screen, make an end stop.

▶ The garden is completed with the addition of a group of three stones and one solitary, larger stone at a distance. The number four is considered unlucky in Japan, so four stones would never be placed together.

▼ The glass tree in this garden is a postcard stand with added glass beads.

This little garden is restful to arrange, beautiful to look at, and could equally fit outside a modern Western home. Use different colours of real gravel, tiny stones or florists' coloured sand. Alternatively, experiment with pulses: try using dried beans, brown rice or red or green lentils. The black 'pebbles' I used are puy lentils.

Divide the area into strips with ½in (13mm) wide stripwood painted black. Spread white PVC wood glue over each strip in turn, and then adhere the surface of your choice, pressing down firmly to produce a neat, flat surface.

A GLASS GARDEN

Clear glass is the latest material to replace gravel in some modern garden designs. Crushed glass for a miniature garden is easy to obtain and costs nothing. Next time you find evidence of a car shunt at the edge of the pavement (sidewalk), gather up the scattered glass – the type used for car windscreens does not splinter and is not sharp (but look carefully to make sure there is no bottle glass among it).

Small glass pebbles (from gift and candle shops) will make good stepping stones, and a large multicoloured glass paperweight or candleholder can be placed strategically to make a feature. The ultra-modern garden is divided with screens that conceal or reveal objects or vistas: the green glass screens used in my garden are photograph frames.

◀ Coloured glass pebbles and a candleholder with a stained-glass top can be incorporated into the garden.

◀ Crushed glass and ring stands make a striking central feature.

A STONE GARDEN

The stone garden is economical with materials and straightforward to arrange: the trick is to create a satisfying pattern with the stones, which may take longer than expected.

The colours and smooth shapes of sea-worn stones are a source of endless fascination. If, like me, you cannot resist collecting tiny pebbles from the seaside, they can be used to make a contemplative Zen garden similar to this one. They need not be fixed down and can be rearranged to suit your mood.

Make a base for the garden from rough-textured, stone-coloured card, and arrange a pattern of differently coloured pebbles. Add a few larger stones and a simple sculpture as a centrepiece.

▼ The oddly shaped 'stone' in the background is a piece of polished coral; the huge rock is a candleholder, containing a few flowers to provide a splash of colour.

▲Contrasting textures and colours show up particularly well on the pale background.

A MOSAIC GARDEN

A brightly coloured garden that glitters is attractive and, above all, fun. Make a base of bright green lawn grass (from a model shop). Edge the inside of the garden box with a hedge of cut, green pan cleaners and cover the outer edges with velvet ribbon.

Make a centrepiece with a coaster of tiny mosaic, and use mosaic tiles to arrange a path. These are available in small sizes from tile and DIY shops – and sometimes in small quantities as free samples.

To extend the garden you can, if you wish, add screens made of brightly coloured thick card behind the box container. Arrange them in series with cut-out spaces and garden pictures placed behind to suggest vistas. Magazines feature beautiful garden pictures which look three-dimensional and realistic when seen through an opening.

▼ Glass and metal earring stands and children's glittery hair ties simulate sparkling trees.

▲ Selecting the materials to make the mosaic garden was a very enjoyable project.

AT THE SEASIDE

A seaside scene is another way to extend the dolls' house with an outdoor setting. A terrace with a view is an attractive option with all sorts of possibilities. Take inspiration from your local seaside resort or a destination that you would like to visit: you may already have brochures as reference.

The view can be of sea only, or can include a distant resort scene with elegant buildings. This seaside terrace has a distinctly tropical feeling.

MAKE A SEASIDE TERRACE

1 First, make a two-sided setting for the scene from foamboard.

a) Cut out a base 17in (430mm) long x 8in (205mm) wide. Mark out an area 12in (305mm) long for the terrace: the remaining 5in (130mm) at the open end will become a small harbour.

b) Cut an end wall 8in (205mm) W x 9in (230mm) H, and a back wall approximately 6in (155mm) L x 9in (230mm) H, plus a 2in (50mm) D extension at the top to make a frame for the view. (Note: the length of the back wall can be adjusted according to the size of 'view' you intend to fit. Measure your chosen picture against the base to check.)

c) Glue the back and side wall to the base.

2 Paint the side and back wall plus the extension in a suitable seaside colour or, alternatively, glue it on to art card to avoid painting.

3 To represent sand, paint the base a sand colour with some interior filler mixed in to give it texture, or use a ready-textured paint sample.

4 Add a bamboo mat to make a seating area next to the walls.

5 Provide a canopy over the seating area: I used a piece of polystyrene packaging with a fancy edge. Alternatively, use a shallow box lid, which can be painted or covered with blue and white striped cotton.

6 Glue your selected 'view' on to stiff card and then fix as an extension to the back wall – overlap the wall by about 2in (50mm) at the back.

Frame the view with ½in (13mm) stripwood, stained natural oak to resemble the colour of driftwood.

7 Paint the harbour area or, alternatively, glue on a picture of calm sea. Edge the beach terrace with fancy stripwood and then edge the whole scene with a thicker stripwood to make a neat finish.

8 Finish the scene with a scattering of tiny shells and a rock or two. I reinforced the tropical effect of my terrace with two dried palm leaves attached to the top of the back wall – they came from a spray of dried leaves. Put a small boat in the harbour: inexpensive models can be found in most toy or model shops.

THE BEACH

A beach scene has all sorts of possibilities. My beach scene is typically British, and includes realistic child dolls to provide a summer holiday atmosphere. The smaller scene includes a rowing boat and fishing tackle, and could be on the Atlantic coast.

Plan the size of the beach carefully, depending on what you want to include, and arrange it in a shallow box lid. Make a low 'sea wall' from stripwood and cover it with stone paper to conceal the edges of the box lid base.

Paint the beach a sand colour. When dry, brush on some PVA white wood glue randomly and cover with florists' sandy gravel. It will look more realistic if this only covers part of the base, not as a thick layer all over. Add some rocks, and then have fun arranging the accessories.

▶ A lunch break for the fisherman. The low sea wall is of real stone, made by a craftsman who builds full-size drystone walls, while the lighthouse came from a shop that specializes in nautical souvenirs.

▼ A beach hut, realistic child dolls, deckchairs and a picnic make the perfect beach holiday scene.

POSTSCRIPT – 2002

To end, I decided to commemorate two events that gave great pleasure to many people during 2002.

The World Cup involved football fans across the globe. In both England and America, football fever was at a high, before, sadly, both teams were knocked out long before the Final. But there is always another time…

Queen Elizabeth's Golden Jubilee was celebrated in Britain and televised in many other countries. This, too, serves as an example of a shared international experience that may inspire your own future project.

Although both these scenes are linked to specific past events, they could be adapted to commemorate something which will give you some personal happy memories, such as the day your team won the cricket match or baseball game, or the annual church fête.

◀ The World Cup scene is set in a typical English pub (public house) that has been specially decorated for the occasion. There is plenty to drink, and the television viewers will shortly drown their sorrows while they discuss what might have been.

◀ My Jubilee scene is a country fête with everything that that implies – a tombola, a maypole, darts and a pig for the Guess the Weight of The Pig competition. Weather permitting, everyone will have a good time.

SUPPLIERS

Dijon Ltd.
The Old Printworks
Streatfield Road
Heathfield
Sussex
TN21 8LA
Tel: 01435 864155
Fax: 01435 865108
email: info@dijon.co.uk
www.dijon.co.uk
(*Colour catalogue available*)

The Dolls House Emporium
High Holborn Road
Ripley,
Derbyshire
DE5 3YD
Freephone: 0800 0523 643
Fax: +44 (0)1773 513 772
Overseas orders
(including Channel Isles and Eire): +44 (0)1773 514 424
www.dollshouse.com
(*Free colour catalogue*)

London Dolls House Company
29 Covent Garden Market
London
WC2E 8RE
Tel: +44 (0)20 7240 8681
www.londondollshouse.co.uk
(*Colour catalogue available*)

Carol Black Miniatures (Mail Order)
Tel: +44 (0)1931 712330
Fax: +44 (0)1931 712990
email: Cblack@breathemail.net
(*Colour catalogue available*)

The Heritage Doll Company
Tel/fax: +44 (0)1206 306201
email: joannawestbrook@supanet.com.
(*Colour catalogue available*)

Margaret's Miniatures of Warminster
Tel: +44 (0)1985 846797
Fax: +44 (0)1985 846796
(*Colour catalogue available*)

Caroline Nevill Miniatures of Bath
Tel/fax: +44 (0)1225 443091

Small Sorts of Salisbury
Tel: +44 (0)1722 337235
(*Colour catalogue available*)

A Woman's Touch
Tel: +44 (0)1782 320078
Fax: +44 (0)1985 846796
email: r.munday1@ntlworld.com
(*Colour catalogue available*)

MAKERS OF FEATURED MINIATURES

BIBLIOGRAPHY

BATTERSBY, Martin. *The Decorative Twenties (revised)*
The Herbert Press, 1988

BATTERSBY, Martin. *The Decorative Thirties (revised)*
Whitney Library of Design NY, 1988

BAYER, Patricia. *Art Deco Architecture*
Thames & Hudson, 1999

BÉDOYÈRE, Guy de la. *The Home Front*
Shire Publications, 2002

BLAKE, Fanny. *Essential Charles Rennie Mackintosh*
Parragon, 2001

COLLINS, David. *New Hotel: architecture and design*
Conran Octopus, 2001

CONRAN, Terence. *Restaurants* Conran Octopus, 2000

CONRAN, Terence. *Small Spaces*
Conran Octopus, 2001

COSTANTINO, Maria. *Art Nouveau* Bison Books, 1989

CUMMING, Elizabeth and KAPLAN, Wendy. *The Arts and Crafts Movement* Thames & Hudson (ppbk World of Art series), 1991

FIELL, Charlotte and Peter (Eds). *50s Decorative Art*
Taschen, 2001

FIELL, Charlotte and Peter (Eds). *70s Decorative Art*
Taschen, 2001

FREEMAN, Michael (photographs) and NOSÉ, Michiko Rico (text). *The Modern Japanese Garden*
Mitchell Beazley, 2002

HENDERSON, Justin. *Museum Architecture*
Rockport Publishers Inc, USA, 1998

HOCKMAN, Hilary. *Edwardian House Style*
David & Charles, 1994

HOPPEN, Kelly. *East Meets West*
Conran Octopus (ppbk), 2001

JACKSON, Lesley. *The Sixties* Phaidon (ppbk), 2000

LEMME, Van De Arie. *A Guide to Art Deco Style*
Apple Press (Quintet Publishing) (reprint), 1988

MATHER, Christine and WOODS, Sharon. *Santa Fe Style* Rizzoli International Pubs NY (ppbk), 1986

MUSGRAVE, Toby. *Courtyard Gardens* Aurum Press Ltd (Jacqui Small imprint), 2001

POSSENTI, Georgie (photographs) and BOISI, Antonells (text). *Living in Sidney* Taschen, 2001

SLESIN, Suzanne, CLIFF, Strafford and ROZENSZTROCH, Daniel. *Japanese Style* Thames & Hudson, 1987 (reprinted 1993)

SLESSOR, Catherine. *See-Through Houses*
Ryland Peters & Small NY, 2001

STEVENSON, Greg. *The 1930s House*
Shire Publications (ppbk), 2000

TOY, Maggie. *Practically Minimal*
Thames & Hudson, 2000

TROCME, Suzanne. *Retro Home* Mitchell Beazley, 2000

WEAVING, Andrew. *Understanding Modern*
Quadrille Publishing, 2001

WEBB, Michael. *Modernism Reborn*
Universe Publishing NY, 2001

WELSH, John. *Modern House* Phaidon (ppbk), 1999

ABOUT THE AUTHOR

Jean Nisbett began to take notice of period houses, their decoration and furniture before she was ten years old, and they have been a consuming passion ever since. She turned this interest to the miniature scale while bringing up a family.

Her work has been shown on BBC Television, Channel 4, UK Style and TF1 France. She began writing while working in the London offices of an American advertising agency, and she is well known as the leading British writer in the dolls' house field. Her articles have appeared regularly in the specialist dolls' house magazines since 1985, as well as in home decoration magazines. This is her sixth book for GMC Publications.

Jean lives in Bath, Somerset.

INDEX

TITLES AVAILABLE FROM
GMC Publications
BOOKS

WOODCARVING

Beginning Woodcarving — *GMC Publications*
Carving Architectural Detail in Wood: The Classical Tradition — *Frederick Wilbur*
Carving Birds & Beasts — *GMC Publications*
Carving the Human Figure: Studies in Wood and Stone — *Dick Onians*
Carving Nature: Wildlife Studies in Wood — *Frank Fox-Wilson*
Celtic Carved Lovespoons: 30 Patterns — *Sharon Littley & Clive Griffin*
Decorative Woodcarving (New Edition) — *Jeremy Williams*
Elements of Woodcarving — *Chris Pye*
Figure Carving in Wood: Human and Animal Forms — *Sara Wilkinson*
Lettercarving in Wood: A Practical Course — *Chris Pye*
Relief Carving in Wood: A Practical Introduction — *Chris Pye*
Woodcarving for Beginners — *GMC Publications*
Woodcarving Made Easy — *Cynthia Rogers*
Woodcarving Tools, Materials & Equipment (New Edition in 2 vols.) — *Chris Pye*

WOODTURNING

Bowl Turning Techniques Masterclass — *Tony Boase*
Chris Child's Projects for Woodturners — *Chris Child*
Decorating Turned Wood: The Maker's Eye — *Liz & Michael O'Donnell*
Green Woodwork — *Mike Abbott*
Keith Rowley's Woodturning Projects — *Keith Rowley*
Making Screw Threads in Wood — *Fred Holder*
Segmented Turning: A Complete Guide — *Ron Hampton*
Turned Boxes: 50 Designs — *Chris Stott*
Turning Green Wood — *Michael O'Donnell*
Turning Pens and Pencils — *Kip Christensen & Rex Burningham*
Woodturning: Forms and Materials — *John Hunnex*
Woodturning: A Foundation Course (New Edition) — *Keith Rowley*
Woodturning: A Fresh Approach — *Robert Chapman*
Woodturning: An Individual Approach — *Dave Regester*
Woodturning: A Source Book of Shapes — *John Hunnex*
Woodturning Masterclass — *Tony Boase*

WOODWORKING

Beginning Picture Marquetry — *Lawrence Threadgold*
Celtic Carved Lovespoons: 30 Patterns — *Sharon Littley & Clive Griffin*
Celtic Woodcraft — *Glenda Bennett*
Complete Woodfinishing (Revised Edition) — *Ian Hosker*
David Charlesworth's Furniture-Making Techniques — *David Charlesworth*
David Charlesworth's Furniture-Making Techniques – Volume 2 — *David Charlesworth*
Furniture Projects with the Router — *Kevin Ley*
Furniture Restoration (Practical Crafts) — *Kevin Jan Bonner*

Furniture Restoration: A Professional at Work — *John Lloyd*
Green Woodwork — *Mike Abbott*
Intarsia: 30 Patterns for the Scrollsaw — *John Everett*
Making Heirloom Boxes — *Peter Lloyd*
Making Screw Threads in Wood — *Fred Holder*
Making Woodwork Aids and Devices — *Robert Wearing*
Mastering the Router — *Ron Fox*
Pine Furniture Projects for the Home — *Dave Mackenzie*
Router Magic: Jigs, Fixtures and Tricks to Unleash your Router's Full Potential — *Bill Hylton*
Router Projects for the Home — *GMC Publications*
Router Tips & Techniques — *Robert Wearing*
Routing: A Workshop Handbook — *Anthony Bailey*
Routing for Beginners — *Anthony Bailey*
Stickmaking: A Complete Course — *Andrew Jones & Clive George*
Stickmaking Handbook — *Andrew Jones & Clive George*
Storage Projects for the Router — *GMC Publications*
Veneering: A Complete Course — *Ian Hosker*
Veneering Handbook — *Ian Hosker*
Woodworking Techniques and Projects — *Anthony Bailey*
Woodworking with the Router: Professional Router Techniques any Woodworker can Use — *Bill Hylton & Fred Matlack*

UPHOLSTERY

Upholstery: A Complete Course (Revised Edition) — *David James*
Upholstery Restoration — *David James*
Upholstery Techniques & Projects — *David James*
Upholstery Tips and Hints — *David James*

DOLLS' HOUSES AND MINIATURES

1/12 Scale Character Figures for the Dolls' House — *James Carrington*
Americana in 1/12 Scale: 50 Authentic Projects — *Joanne Ogreenc & Mary Lou Santovec*
The Authentic Georgian Dolls' House — *Brian Long*
A Beginners' Guide to the Dolls' House Hobby — *Jean Nisbett*
Celtic, Medieval and Tudor Wall Hangings in 1/12 Scale Needlepoint — *Sandra Whitehead*
Creating Decorative Fabrics: Projects in 1/12 Scale — *Janet Storey*
Dolls' House Accessories, Fixtures and Fittings — *Andrea Barham*
Dolls' House Furniture: Easy-to-Make Projects in 1/12 Scale — *Freida Gray*
Dolls' House Makeovers — *Jean Nisbett*
Dolls' House Window Treatments — *Eve Harwood*
Edwardian-Style Hand-Knitted Fashion for 1/12 Scale Dolls — *Yvonne Wakefield*
How to Make Your Dolls' House Special: Fresh Ideas for Decorating — *Beryl Armstrong*

CRAFTS

GARDENING

Marginal Plants — *Bernard Sleeman*
Orchids are Easy: A Beginner's Guide to their Care and Cultivation — *Tom Gilland*
Planting Plans for Your Garden — *Jenny Shukman*
Sink and Container Gardening Using Dwarf Hardy Plants — *Chris & Valerie Wheeler*
The Successful Conservatory and Growing Exotic Plants — *Joan Phelan*
Success with Cuttings — *Chris & Valerie Wheeler*
Success with Seeds — *Chris & Valerie Wheeler*
Tropical Garden Style with Hardy Plants — *Alan Hemsley*
Water Garden Projects: From Groundwork to Planting — *Roger Sweetinburgh*

PHOTOGRAPHY

Close-Up on Insects — *Robert Thompson*
Digital Enhancement for Landscape Photographers — *Arjan Hoogendam & Herb Parkin*
Double Vision — *Chris Weston & Nigel Hicks*
An Essential Guide to Bird Photography — *Steve Young*
Field Guide to Bird Photography — *Steve Young*
Field Guide to Landscape Photography — *Peter Watson*
How to Photograph Pets — *Nick Ridley*
In my Mind's Eye: Seeing in Black and White — *Charlie Waite*
Life in the Wild: A Photographer's Year — *Andy Rouse*
Light in the Landscape: A Photographer's Year — *Peter Watson*
Photographers on Location with Charlie Waite — *Charlie Waite*
Photography for the Naturalist — *Mark Lucock*
Photojournalism: An Essential Guide — *David Herrod*
Professional Landscape and Environmental Photography:
From 35mm to Large Format — *Mark Lucock*

Rangefinder — *Roger Hicks & Frances Schultz*
Underwater Photography — *Paul Kay*
Where and How to Photograph Wildlife — *Peter Evans*
Wildlife Photography Workshops — *Steve & Ann Toon*

ART TECHNIQUES

Oil Paintings from your Garden: A Guide for Beginners — *Rachel Shirley*

VIDEOS

Drop-in and Pinstuffed Seats — *David James*
Stuffover Upholstery — *David James*
Elliptical Turning — *David Springett*
Woodturning Wizardry — *David Springett*
Turning Between Centres: The Basics — *Dennis White*
Turning Bowls — *Dennis White*
Boxes, Goblets and Screw Threads — *Dennis White*
Novelties and Projects — *Dennis White*
Classic Profiles — *Dennis White*
Twists and Advanced Turning — *Dennis White*
Sharpening the Professional Way — *Jim Kingshott*
Sharpening Turning & Carving Tools — *Jim Kingshott*
Bowl Turning — *John Jordan*
Hollow Turning — *John Jordan*
Woodturning: A Foundation Course — *Keith Rowley*
Carving a Figure: The Female Form — *Ray Gonzalez*
The Router: A Beginner's Guide — *Alan Goodsell*
The Scroll Saw: A Beginner's Guide — *John Burke*

MAGAZINES

WOODTURNING ✦ WOODCARVING ✦ FURNITURE & CABINETMAKING
THE ROUTER ✦ NEW WOODWORKING ✦ THE DOLLS' HOUSE MAGAZINE
OUTDOOR PHOTOGRAPHY ✦ BLACK & WHITE PHOTOGRAPHY
MACHINE KNITTING NEWS ✦ KNITTING
GUILD OF MASTER CRAFTSMEN NEWS

The above represents a full list of all titles currently published or scheduled to be published.
All are available direct from the Publishers or through bookshops, newsagents and specialist retailers.
To place an order, or to obtain a complete catalogue, contact:

GMC Publications,
Castle Place, 166 High Street, Lewes, East Sussex BN7 1XU United Kingdom
Tel: 01273 488005 Fax: 01273 402866
E-mail: pubs@thegmcgroup.com

Orders by credit card are accepted